Film Music: A Very Short Introduction

VERY SHORT INTRODUCTIONS are for anyone wanting a stimulating and accessible way into a new subject. They are written by experts, and have been translated into more than 45 different languages.

The series began in 1995, and now covers a wide variety of topics in every discipline. The VSI library currently contains over 700 volumes—a Very Short Introduction to everything from Psychology and Philosophy of Science to American History and Relativity—and continues to grow in every subject area.

Very Short Introductions available now:

ABOLITIONISM Richard S. Newman
THE ABRAHAMIC RELIGIONS
 Charles L. Cohen
ACCOUNTING Christopher Nobes
ADDICTION Keith Humphreys
ADOLESCENCE Peter K. Smith
THEODOR W. ADORNO
 Andrew Bowie
ADVERTISING Winston Fletcher
AERIAL WARFARE Frank Ledwidge
AESTHETICS Bence Nanay
AFRICAN AMERICAN HISTORY
 Jonathan Scott Holloway
AFRICAN AMERICAN RELIGION
 Eddie S. Glaude Jr.
AFRICAN HISTORY John Parker
 and Richard Rathbone
AFRICAN POLITICS Ian Taylor
AFRICAN RELIGIONS Jacob K. Olupona
AGEING Nancy A. Pachana
AGNOSTICISM Robin Le Poidevin
AGRICULTURE Paul Brassley
 and Richard Soffe
ALEXANDER THE GREAT
 Hugh Bowden
ALGEBRA Peter M. Higgins
AMERICAN BUSINESS HISTORY
 Walter A. Friedman
AMERICAN CULTURAL HISTORY
 Eric Avila
AMERICAN FOREIGN RELATIONS
 Andrew Preston
AMERICAN HISTORY Paul S. Boyer
AMERICAN IMMIGRATION
 David A. Gerber

AMERICAN INTELLECTUAL HISTORY
 Jennifer Ratner-Rosenhagen
THE AMERICAN JUDICIAL SYSTEM
 Charles L. Zelden
AMERICAN LEGAL HISTORY
 G. Edward White
AMERICAN MILITARY HISTORY
 Joseph T. Glatthaar
AMERICAN NAVAL HISTORY
 Craig L. Symonds
AMERICAN POETRY David Caplan
AMERICAN POLITICAL HISTORY
 Donald Critchlow
AMERICAN POLITICAL PARTIES
 AND ELECTIONS L. Sandy Maisel
AMERICAN POLITICS
 Richard M. Valelly
THE AMERICAN PRESIDENCY
 Charles O. Jones
THE AMERICAN REVOLUTION
 Robert J. Allison
AMERICAN SLAVERY
 Heather Andrea Williams
THE AMERICAN SOUTH
 Charles Reagan Wilson
THE AMERICAN WEST Stephen Aron
AMERICAN WOMEN'S HISTORY
 Susan Ware
AMPHIBIANS T. S. Kemp
ANAESTHESIA Aidan O'Donnell
ANALYTIC PHILOSOPHY
 Michael Beaney
ANARCHISM Alex Prichard
ANCIENT ASSYRIA Karen Radner
ANCIENT EGYPT Ian Shaw

Available soon:

For more information visit our website

www.oup.com/vsi/

Kathryn Kalinak

FILM MUSIC

A Very Short Introduction

SECOND EDITION

OXFORD
UNIVERSITY PRESS

OXFORD
UNIVERSITY PRESS

Oxford University Press is a department of the University of Oxford.
It furthers the University's objective of excellence in research, scholarship,
and education by publishing worldwide. Oxford is a registered trade mark of
Oxford University Press in the UK and in certain other countries.

Published in the United States of America by Oxford University Press
198 Madison Avenue, New York, NY 10016, United States of America.

© Oxford University Press 2010, 2023

Library of Congress Cataloging-in-Publication Data

Names: Kalinak, Kathryn Marie, 1952- author.
Title: Film music : a very short introduction / Kathryn Kalinak.
Description: Second edition. | New York : Oxford University Press, 2023. |
Series: Very short introductions
Identifiers: LCCN 2023013817 (print) |
LCCN 2023013818 (ebook) | ISBN 9780197628034 (paperback) |
ISBN 9780197628058 (epub)
Subjects: LCSH: Motion picture music—History and criticism.
Classification: LCC ML2075 .K33 2023 (print) | LCC ML2075 (ebook) |
DDC 781.5/42—dc23/eng/20230322
LC record available at https://lccn.loc.gov/2023013817
LC ebook record available at https://lccn.loc.gov/2023013818

1 3 5 7 9 8 6 4 2

Printed and bound by
CPI Group (UK) Ltd, Croydon, CR0 4YY

Contents

List of illustrations

Preface to the second edition

Film music is music that is either directly composed or expressly chosen to accompany a motion picture. As a practice, it is as old as cinema itself—the very first projected images in many places around the globe either captured a musical performance or were accompanied by one. In places where accompaniment did not initially attend motion pictures, it would soon do so. Film music has been both live and recorded, both newly composed and compiled from existing sources, both meticulously orchestrated and spontaneously produced through improvisation. It does not operate in exactly the same way across time, across cultures, and sometimes even within cultures. Across the board, however, it is characterized by its power to define meaning and to express emotion: film music guides our response to the images and connects us to them.

As I wrote this second edition, I found that some things about film music had not changed—its definition, for instance. But some things have. Since the first edition of this book was published in 2010, there has appeared significant new work on film music as it is practiced globally. Hollywood film music has played an oversized role in the history, theory, and criticism of film music; as a result, film music outside Hollywood has been underresearched. In the preface to the first edition I wrote, "I have tried to focus on the major film industries around the world but even this endeavor has been limited by the lack of information about film music in some of the world's largest industries." It has been a pleasure, in the past decade, to see that information emerge in exciting new work in English on film music in Argentina, Australia, Austria, Belgium, Brazil, China, Cuba, Democratic Republic of Congo, France, Germany, Hong Kong, Iran, Ireland, Italy, Japan, Korea, Mexico, Mongolia, New Zealand, Portugal, Russia, Senegal, Spain, Sweden, Taiwan, Turkey, Ukraine, and Bollywood, Kollywood, and Nollywood, the Hindi, Tamil, and Nigerian film industries, respectively. There has also been the welcome production of several comprehensive bibliographies on film music, including one devoted to its global practice, *Music and Cinema, Global Practices*, in the Oxford Online Bibliographies series.

This second edition also updates the coverage to 2022. In the first chapter, "What does film music do?," which serves as a crash course in the functions of film music, the analysis of a cue from *Reservoir Dogs* (1992) has been replaced with one from *The Shape of Water* (2017). The three film music history chapters have been restructured to accommodate the additional decade. The final chapter, "Composers and their craft," has been expanded to include noteworthy work since 2010 and features new names. Some live and work globally. Others have historically lacked access to film scoring. They are starting to make an impact.

As in the first edition, I follow the practice of the *Oxford History of World Cinema* with respect to film titles. When an English-language title is available, it is used. Films known uniquely or only by a foreign-language title are referred to in the original language. Names follow Western practice. Suggestions in the Further Reading and Recommended Viewing sections have been updated through 2022.

What has not changed is this book's purpose: it is still designed to serve as a general introduction to the subject, with an overview of film music from the theoretical to the pragmatic and from the sweep of history to the role of the individual. As was true for the first edition, although it includes references to film music as music, this book is not a specialized study of music and readers need no prior musical training to enjoy it. It was written to be clear and accessible to the general reader.

Chapter 1
What does film music do?

What does film music do? Since many in the audience do not even hear it, what good is it? I would like to begin to answer these questions by looking at film music in action, by analyzing how music, in this case a preexisting song, operates in a sequence from a recent film, *The Shape of Water* (2017). The song featured is "Chica Chica Boom Chic" by Mack Gordon and Harry Warren.

Film music, whether it is a pop song, an improvised accompaniment, or an originally composed cue, can do a variety of things. It can establish setting, specifying a particular time and place; it can fashion a mood and create atmosphere; it can reinforce or foreshadow narrative developments and contribute to the way we respond to them; it can resonate and even create emotion, sometimes only dimly realized in the images, for us to experience; it can elucidate character, fleshing out screen images with personality, background, and motivation; it can help us to know what characters are thinking and feeling; it can encapsulate a film's theme. Film music can unify a series of images that might seem disconnected on their own and impart a rhythm to their unfolding. And while it is doing all of this, film music encourages our absorption into the film by distracting us from its technological basis—its constitution as a series of two-dimensional, larger (or smaller) than life, sometimes black-and-white, and sometimes silent, images. Film music does not do all these things all the time. But music is so useful to film because it can do so much simultaneously.

A multipurpose music cue

Take the preexisting song "Chica Chica Boom Chic," performed by Carmen Miranda and functioning as background score for a montage in *The Shape of Water*. The sequence begins with the boss, Mr. Strickland, driving to work in his new Cadillac and continues with the suspicious activities of the protagonist, Elisa, a cleaner in the experimental lab where Strickland works. Her behavior is definitely noticed by Zelda, her coworker and friend. The sequence ends in Elisa's neighbor's apartment, where, broadcast on a television set, Carmen Miranda appears singing the song in the film in which it originally appeared, *That Night in Rio* (1941). Shortly after this sequence, Elisa reveals her plan to abduct the sea creature trapped in the lab and take him home with her. The music, one of Miranda's signature tunes, initially seems out of place, unrelated to the setting or the mood, the characters, the plot, or the film's theme. But the repurposing of "Chica Chica Boom Chic" in *The Shape of Water* demonstrates how music can bring added dimension to a film, in this case, in some complex ways.

One of film music's primary functions is to create mood, an important component in how an audience responds. The sequence that "Chica Chica Boom Chic" accompanies is a montage. It begins with the crass, narrow-minded, sexist, and predatory boss, Mr. Strickland, driving his new Cadillac to work. The upbeat song telegraphs to the audience the joy he is experiencing and it imparts a light-hearted and fun mood to his drive, adding to the enjoyability of the sequence. But the song is doing more. Film music can also resonate emotion between the screen and the audience. When we recognize an emotion attributed to characters, we become more invested in them. The film feels more immediate, more real. Music is one of the most powerful emotional prompts in film, encouraging us to empathize with onscreen characters, in this case, urging us to share Strickland's joy. Part of that infectious fun is produced by the rhythm of the music, which dictates the editing and lends lyricism and energy to the image track. What is so interesting about this moment is that Strickland is a completely unsympathetic character. Indeed, music is so engaging that it authorizes us to share this creep's joy and experience vicariously his fun in driving and showing off a new car.

The song also provides the soundtrack to Elisa's actions, which follow Strickland's arrival at work. Elisa is scoping out the lab for an escape plan, and her suspicious behavior catches Zelda's attention. From a narrative standpoint, the music helps to alert us to an important plot development, signaling us to pay attention, as Zelda does, to a series of actions that initially seem unconnected. These are the first steps in Elisa's plan to free the sea creature, and thus the sequence foreshadows the dramatic revelation of Elisa's plot later in the film.

This entire sequence, constituted by Strickland's and Elisa's actions, is a montage, a series of images largely without sound effects and dialogue. It is designed to telegraph Elisa's preparations for freeing the sea creature as well as Strickland's complete obliviousness to her plan. Montages are some of film's most precarious moments from a structural standpoint, when the apparatus of filmmaking is the most exposed: How are these shots connected? Why are we not hearing the sounds that are obviously being produced by the images? Why are we hearing only selective dialogue when there is obviously more being produced? Typically, music is foregrounded in a montage, distracting us from these questions and smoothing over the delivery of the image track. Its job, in essence, is to cover gaps in the narrative chain. Music offers its own structure to the montage, imparting unity to a series of disconnected images.

Further, music distracts us from the very nature of film itself—its technological basis as a two-dimensional, sometimes black-and-white, sometimes silent, and larger (or now, smaller) than life series of images designed to produce the impression of reality—to sustain our absorption into the film.

Film music can also provide insight into character psychology and this song has particular importance in relation to Elisa. We know little about her. She is mute and communicates through sign language. We get only glimpses of her inner life through friendships with her neighbor, an artist and cinephile; her coworker, with whom she shares a bond; and the sea creature, whom she eventually comes to love. The songs chosen to accompany her are often revelatory, none more so than "Chica Chica Boom Chic." Created specifically for Carmen Miranda, the song tapped into her fiery persona, the Brazilian Bombshell, the sexy Latina, who danced the samba in unforgettable costumes as she sang. Miranda always played some version of herself, often sang in Portuguese, and typically mangled the English language in comic malapropisms throughout her films (but not in real life). Elisa, shy, reserved, and timid, seems the antithesis of Miranda. And yet, by film's end Elisa has engineered a heroic escape for the sea creature, eluded authorities for weeks, and inaugurated an intense and passionate cross-species love affair. Miranda's song and the evocation of Miranda herself—remember she appears on the television at the sequence's end—beckon us to reconsider what we think we know about Elisa and brings out a layer of her personality—daring, passionate, extraordinary in the best sense of the word—that is not immediately apparent on the image track.

Using a preexisting song in ironic contrast to the image track, as done here in *The Shape of Water*, is not how preexisting music is typically used in soundtracks. But some other recent films offer striking examples: Charlie Chaplin's "Smile" from *Modern Times*

4

(1936) appearing in *Joker* (2018), or the disco classic "It's Raining Men" in *Promising Young Woman* (2020). Stanley Kubrick pioneered the practice in *A Clockwork Orange* (1971), where "Singin' in the Rain" accompanies a graphic murder. But the classic example remains "Stuck in the Middle with You," a bubblegum classic of the 1970s, for the torture sequence in *Reservoir Dogs* (1992).

If we dig a little deeper into "Chica Chica Boom Chic," there is even more for the music to tell us. *That Night in Rio* (1941), where the song first appears, was made in Hollywood after the eruption of war in Europe and with an eye to the new US Good Neighbor Policy aimed at consolidating the support of Latin America for US interests. It stars Miranda as Carmen, a fiery Brazilian, and Don Ameche as Larry, her Anglo boyfriend, as they negotiate the many impediments, largely comic, keeping these lovers from two divergent cultures apart. "Chica Chica Boom Chic" is a duet for Miranda and Ameche as they attempt to bridge their different worlds, musical and otherwise, with Miranda singing in Portuguese (this is the section we hear in *The Shape of Water*) in the rhythmic, animated, and percussive style of samba, followed by Ameche in English singing about improving US relations with South America in a smooth and lyrical baritone in a style developed on Broadway. Miranda challenges him to a sing-off: samba versus Broadway, Bahia (the home of samba) versus Tin Pan Alley (the name by which the New York music publishing industry came to be known). The number ends after a long dance break with the lovers united, hand in hand. For viewers who know the song or look it up on YouTube, "Chica Chica Boom Chic" encapsulates, albeit in a light-hearted way, the conflict at the center of *The Shape of Water*: the collision of two different cultures that the lovers must negotiate. *The Shape of Water* takes this theme to a new level. The lovers come not only from different cultures but also from different species.

The compilation score and the role of the music supervisor

The Shape of Water combines two types of film scores: an original score composed specifically for the film (for which Alexandre Desplat won an Academy Award, known colloquially as an Oscar) and a compilation score consisting of preexisting music chosen or facilitated by a music supervisor (in this case John Houlihan, who is credited as music consultant). Compilation scores have dramatically changed the landscape of film scoring, shifting the responsibility for the music from the composer to the director or the music supervisor, or both. Ultimately, it is the job of the music supervisor to realize the director's vision. First-time director Emerald Fennell created a playlist for *Promising Young Woman*, but it was music supervisor Susan Jacobs who realized it on a miniscule budget and without many of the marquee songs on Fennell's playlist. As Jacobs describes the process, "You're really facilitating somebody with a really clear vision and…helping them to learn to drive."

Many directors are actively involved. Wong Kar-wai did not even have the script for *Chungking Express* (1994) when he described the project to his cinematographer by playing "California Dreamin'," a song that plays a key role in the film. Quentin Tarantino wanted the music for *Once upon a Time in Hollywood* (2019) to be a time capsule of the 1960s and chose all the music accordingly, even including a cue from Bernard Herrmann's discarded score for *Torn Curtain* (1966). According to his long-time music supervisor, Mary Ramos, Tarantino has an entire room devoted to his record collection, and the process starts with him "talking a mile a minute and pausing to put the needle down on records…as I madly scribble." Guillermo del Toro wanted to make the music for *The Shape of Water* "into a songbook of two or three decades" of American music and spent months reviewing thousands of songs. He wrote his choices directly into his screenplay, among them "Chica Chica Boom Chic."

Interestingly, the job of music supervisor has opened up space for women in the Hollywood film music industry. Seven of *Variety*'s list of 10 Music Supervisors to Watch in 2021 are women. At this writing, there is no Academy Award for Music Supervision. But in 2017, the Academy of Television Arts and Sciences awarded its first Emmy for Outstanding Music Supervision to Susan Jacobs.

A final word on how we listen

Film music shapes meaning on a number of levels. Audiences will respond to film music, as they do to film, with varying degrees of awareness. But whether we are consciously aware of it or not, film music can engage us with meanings and pull us toward responses, such as getting us to see Elisa with more dimension, without precisely knowing why. My point here is that the operation of film music often takes place on a less than fully conscious plane. When film music operates under the radar of consciousness, it has intensified power to affect us.

These observations about the function of music in narrative film are not unique to *The Shape of Water*. I chose this example because it demonstrates key properties of film music in a complex way. And although film music is a kind of universal language, it operates differently across time and across cultures. Even so, music has an expressive power that crosses many borders, and film traditions throughout the world have harnessed music's expressive power to shape the perception of film and to reverberate emotion between the spectator and the screen.

Chapter 2
How does film music work?

Film music lies at the intersection of film and music, an obvious enough observation, but probing this intersection fully is crucial to understanding how film music operates. Film music inherits one part of its ability to make meaning from its constitution as a musical practice and another part from its constitution as a cinematic practice. Although it is often recorded or performed, marketed, and heard purely as music, film music is nevertheless defined by its function within a cinematic field of reference. Thus, music in film is always something of a hybrid.

Film music as a musical practice

This book is not intended as a specialized study of music, and it requires no musical training on the part of its readers. But film music is, after all, music, and like any meaning system, it depends on certain forms and structures, as well as the patterns of meaning contained in them, to make it intelligible. Just as we learn to read a film, that is, to connect specific meanings to the various techniques at the filmmaker's disposal (such as an editing dissolve, which tells us that time has passed), so, too, we can learn to read music, that is, to recognize the basic building blocks of music (such as tonality, melody, harmony, rhythm, tempo, dynamics, timbre, instrumentation, and form) at the disposal of the composer and connect specific meanings to them. If this process seems more intimidating for music than for film, it may be that our more extended acquaintance with visual media has made reading images seem easier. But remember that we had to learn to read films, too.

Although music is universal (all human cultures that have left records appear to have produced it), music is by no means a universal language shared among all people across time. Throughout human history, music has been constituted in a myriad of ways. The music of the Western world, as it coalesced around a set of principles in the early modern period, is but one of them. It provides a useful entry point into understanding film music, however, for a variety of reasons. Western music exerted a powerful influence globally in the late nineteenth and early twentieth centuries at the very moment when film music was developing; thus it played a large part in the history of musical accompaniment around the world. And it is the musical system with which most English speakers will be familiar. Obviously, music exists outside the Western world. This book includes numerous examples from non-Western musics that will function as a contrapuntal voice as well as a reminder that Western music is only one kind of music among many worldwide.

The basic building blocks of Western music hinge on tonality, a structure for organizing musical sounds into music. Tonality may be defined as a musical system revolving around a single tone or note that functions as a center of gravity: it is a focal point around which the rest of the notes are organized and which serves as the place where a piece of music begins and ends. Classical Indian music and many kinds of Middle Eastern music that are based in tonality depend on a single tone droned throughout an entire piece to provide a stable tonal base. Western music works in a different way, producing tension and release as the music moves alternatively away from and toward a tonal center. Western tonality is divided between major and minor modes that can carry specific associations and distinct inflections. While there is nothing inherently happy or sad about music composed in a major or minor mode, associations of happiness and brightness are often attached to the major mode, while associations of melancholy and ominousness are often attached to the minor. Of course, there are plenty of exceptions. "My Favorite Things" from Richard Rodgers and Oscar Hammerstein's *The Sound of Music* is written in the minor, for instance.

A distinguishing characteristic of tonal music, since about the middle of the eighteenth century, is the privileging of melody, a series of notes played in a memorable and recognizable order. Melody provides an access point into music, a hook on which to hang listeners' attention. Western music is not alone in utilizing melody. Classical Indian music, for instance, is built on melodies that have coalesced over centuries into a body of recognizable and commonly shared rāgas, each with a unique melodic pattern and a fixed association such as tranquility, heroism, power, or pathos. Thus film composers in India, both in the traditional background score and in film songs, can easily access powerful musical structures for creating mood and atmosphere through the use of rāgas.

Film composers around the globe have engaged melody. The Bollywood composer A. R. Rahman credits melody with "a very important role in my sensibility in music." Melody, however, has been a hallmark of Hollywood scoring. John Barry explains, "I love working with melody. I think if you can capture something in the simplest possible way, which is what melody is, then you're halfway there." Randy Newman claims, "I believe in melody. Maybe there are places where you don't want it, but I don't know where they'd be." Melody has often taken the form of a leitmotif, an identifiable and recurring musical pattern. A leitmotif can consist of any kind of musical material—a distinctive rhythm, for instance—but Hollywood composers have tended to construct leitmotifs through melody, either as short as a motif of a few notes or as extended as a theme. Leitmotifs can be developed and varied throughout the score (or repeated verbatim), reinforcing associations and becoming more and more powerful as a film progresses. The final reiteration of a leitmotif—especially when it coincides with the end of a film—can have an enormous emotional impact. Still, not all Hollywood composers privilege melody—just try humming the shower sequence from Bernard Herrmann's score for *Psycho* (1960)—but melody is nonetheless a powerful tool for shaping a score.

Harmony has to do with the coordination of notes playing simultaneously. In Western tonal music, harmony privileges certain combinations of notes, or chords, over others, creating stress points built on dissonance and resolutions that dissipate dissonance. The farther harmony moves from the tonal center, the more associations of disorder and instability will be activated; the closer to the tonal center, the more associations of order and stability. Harmony is often less immediately recognizable than melody, but its effects are powerful and discernible even by those without the language to describe them.

Interestingly, harmony is not a requirement of music, and many musical practices throughout history and around the globe are not harmonic in the way that Western tonal music is. Musical systems that depend on improvisation, such as Indian and Middle Eastern, lack a focus on harmony in the Western sense, and early music from many places around the globe, including the West, do not depend on it. And the set of seven tones or notes that comprise Western music's harmonic system represents only one such organizational structure. The pentatonic scale, used in many Asian and Native American musics, uses five tones. In Mongolia, during the socialist era, filmmakers were charged with elevating socialism and composers with using the Western tonal system sanctioned by the Soviet Union. Mongolian film composers, however, sometimes used the pentatonic scale, the basis of Mongolian traditional music, harmonizing and orchestrating the approved diatonic melodies through the pentatonic mode, surreptitiously defying Soviet authority. The octatonic scale uses eight tones. Jonny Greenwood has used the octatonic scale in *The Power of the Dog* (2021), where he said it can lend "a nice, tense sourness in the middle of all of the sweetness" of a scene.

Rhythm refers to the organization of music through time; its basic unit is the beat, a discernible pulse that marks out the passage of time. Western music is characterized by a high degree of regularity in terms of rhythm, and deviations from established patterns can be very potent. On the one hand, many music systems throughout the world depend on rhythm, although they may operate differently than in Western music. In Indian music, musical rhythms have coalesced into established patterns far more complicated than Western rhythms. In Western music, a rhythm can be established in as few as three or four beats. One traditional Indian rhythmic pattern comprises 108 separate beats before it repeats. Middle Eastern song practice, on the other hand, often depends not on regular rhythms but on flexible rhythms that can adjust to the lyrics. In Western tonal music, rhythm is much more predictable, operating as a sonic grid against which the composer writes.

Timbre refers to the quality of sound that distinguishes one instrument or voice from another. To hear timbre in action, we might think of the difference in Western music between concert music and popular music traditions. Concert music aims to produce a fairly standard timbre within a vocal range or class of instruments (which can make it difficult to distinguish one operatic soprano from another). Popular music, however, aims in the opposite direction, to distinguish one voice from another, one way of playing an instrument from another. Establishing a unique timbre is one way of doing so, and most listeners can probably tell the difference between Mariah Carey and P!nk. Timbre is a powerful worldwide musical property. It is of great importance to Japanese music, for instance, where singers and instrumentalists are trained to create a multiplicity of different timbres with the same instrument or voice. Traditional *Gidayu-bushi* singers can even customize the timbre of their voices to establish gender and age. In certain African musical traditions, the timbre of a voice is individuated by extramusical properties that many other vocal traditions attempt to minimize, such as the sound of breathing. Instrumentation can be thought of as the art of selecting different timbres, choosing one instrument or voice over another to create specific effects, using violins instead of horns, for example, or a bass voice over a tenor voice.

Listening for all these musical properties while you watch a film may seem like a very tall order—and I have not even included all the musical tools at the disposal of the composer (tempo, dynamics, and musical form are obvious omissions). One of the best and easiest ways to hear these properties is through musical conventions that harness musical affects to specific meanings through the power of association. Musical conventions become ingrained in a culture and function as a kind of musical collective unconscious, affecting listeners whether or not they are consciously aware of them. Think of musical conventions as a cultural shorthand that does not have to be consciously recognized by listeners to produce predictable responses. For obvious reasons, film composers depend on musical conventions to guide and control audience response, but composers can also deliberately contradict these conventions for dramatic effect. Musical conventions do not function universally. They change across history and are culturally determined. What works at one point in time and in one place on the globe may not in another. In Hollywood, brass instruments have conventionally connoted heroism, but in Hindi film, brasses often signify villainy. Still, musical conventions can produce predictable audience reactions and are frequently exploited to direct an audience's emotional and psychological trajectory through a film by composers working both within Western music and outside it.

For example, in Disney's animated feature *Beauty and the Beast* (1991), Alan Menken and Howard Ashman created the song "Beauty and the Beast" to function as a love theme for Belle and the Beast. The song is based on well-established conventions for romantic passion: a major key, stable harmonies, a prominent use of violins (commonly thought of as the most expressive instrument in the orchestra and thus linked to passion), and a memorable melody with upward leaps in the melodic pattern. These conventions are so powerful that they connote romance whether or not an audience consciously recognizes their use. In this instance, lyrics emphasize these musical conventions: "Tale as old as time, song as old as rhyme." But even without the lyrics, the song has tapped into musical conventions for romance that are among the most identifiable (and some might add shopworn) strategies in Hollywood film scoring.

Musical conventions can help to create a variety of moods and emotions. One of the most famous film music cues is the one Bernard Herrmann composed for the shower sequence in *Psycho*. Herrmann exploited a number of musical conventions for invoking terror: the absence of melody, unpredictable rhythms, strident and dissonant harmonies, violins at the very top and basses at the very bottom of their ranges played with techniques that inhibit lyricism. Interestingly, Herrmann's shower cue has become such an iconic musical creation of terror that its distinctive shrieking violins have now become a convention for terror itself, evoked in countless horror films, parodies of horror films, television shows, and perhaps the real horror, television commercials.

Contemporary film composers in Hollywood have begun to tap into conventions of world music to guide and shape audience response. For Mira Nair's *Monsoon Wedding* (2001), Mychael Danna created the main title sequence based on a traditional Indian *baraat*, the wedding processional for the groom. Although there was a great deal of improvisation in the recording of this cue, it is based on a traditional Indian rāga with associations of joy and harmony. As with "Beauty and the Beast," it is not necessary for audiences to be consciously aware of the convention, in this case the identity of the *Rāga Kalyan*, for the music to transmit joy. Indian audiences who recognize the cultural reference will have a deeper experience of the music than audiences who do not, and thus Danna's choice becomes a particularly compelling one, from a multicultural perspective, for a film about India aimed at a global audience.

A film composer can even violate established musical conventions to create intriguing and disturbing effects. Ennio Morricone in *The Good, the Bad, and the Ugly* (1966) used minor keys for many of the fast-paced and thrilling action sequences and major keys for many of the somber and melancholic sequences. Herrmann's cue for *Psycho* is a veritable blueprint for musical terror. At the same time that he invoked conventions for horror, however, Herrmann ignored the most typical convention for creating suspense—tremolo, or rapidly vibrating strings—and deliberately undercut another convention by using violins not for romance but for murder. In fact, the *Psycho* score is composed exclusively for strings.

Film music as a cinematic practice

Our experience of film music is shaped by its constitution as music. But film music does not operate in a vacuum; it functions as part of a larger system of meaning. Film itself is a narrative form. Although there are certainly films that are nonnarrative in their construction, film developed into an art form to tell stories. Music is part of this process, a key part.

Music's function in film preoccupied the earliest critics and scholars of film music. In the 1930s, the first wave of film music criticism began to be published, positing that sound was subordinate to the image. Film music, it was argued, related to the

15

image either through parallelism (reinforcing the image's content) or through counterpoint (contradicting the image's content). This model was influenced, no doubt, by the famous "Statement on Sound," signed by Soviet filmmakers Sergei Eisenstein, Vsevolod Pudovkin, and Grigori Alexandrov in 1928, which categorized film sound according to whether it paralleled or counterpointed the image. Within a decade, the influential critic Theodor Adorno and composer Hanns Eisler, in their groundbreaking *Composing for the Films*, pointed out, "A photographed kiss cannot actually be synchronized with an eight-bar phrase." Adorno and Eisler argued that visual imagery and music are very different forms of expression, and they do not operate, in any sense, in ways that could accurately be described as parallel or contrapuntal.

Further, positing that music either parallels or counterpoints what is already "there" assumes that the image is autonomous and encodes meaning unproblematically. Even in the early twenty-first century some film music criticism continues to employ terminology that assumes the image is the bearer of meaning and that music functions to modify that meaning in some way, heightening, reinforcing, or undercutting what is "in" the image. Because visual images are representational, that is, because on the surface at least, they make direct reference to what they represent, it is easy to assume that visual images have immediate, obvious, and stable meaning. This is not always (or perhaps ever) the case. Visual images can be amorphous and ambiguous, and even the surface of an image can be open to multiple interpretations. It is problematic to assume that meaning is unproblematically "there" in the image.

There are a number of other problems with the parallelism/ counterpoint model. How can we account for film music that neither parallels nor counterpoints the image? I would find it difficult to describe "Chica Chica Boom Chic" in *The Shape of Water* as either paralleling or counterpointing the images. The use of that song is much more complex than either of those two options can account for.

Film is a narrative medium, an art form that delivers stories. The soundtrack and the visual track always operate within this larger field of reference. Contemporary film music scholars have shaped a different model for film music's operation in which music is seen as an interdependent and complementary element of a film's narrative system. Music shares power to create meaning with a number of elements that come together to tell a story, among them mise-en-scène, cinematography, acting, editing, dialogue, and sound. When we hear tremolo strings, it is not a simple case of music reinforcing the suspense that is already there in the image. Instead, tremolo strings are a component of the process by which suspense is generated. The basic elements of film work together in narrative film in a "*combinatoire* of expression," Claudia Gorbman's evocative phrase.

Let's delve a bit more deeply into film music's function in relation to narrative. Roland Barthes's work on the function of photographic captions offers fruitful insight here. Captions control and limit the perception of photographs, a process Barthes called *ancrage* (anchoring). Film music works in the same way, reinforcing one meaning out of many possible meanings, anchoring the image to specificity. It is as if the music "throws a net around the floating visual signifier," in Gorbman's words. And that is what Noel Carroll means when he describes film music's function as "modifying." Just as adjectives and adverbs pin down the meaning of the nouns and verbs they are attached to, film music pins down the image track. Film music polices the ways in which the audience perceives the image and does so in a complex relationship with other elements of a film's narrative system.

Film music works in a network of mutual implication. In the same way that music can anchor the image in specificity, the image can impart explicitness to the music by giving it referentiality, grounding the general expressiveness of the music in a specificity it might not otherwise have had. And music's function in film is always bounded by the limits of credibility itself. Imagine hearing the cue from the shower sequence of *Psycho* as Belle and the Beast dance around the ballroom in *Beauty and the Beast* or the song "Beauty and the Beast" as accompaniment to the grisly shower murder in *Psycho*. The farther music drifts away from mutual dependency with the rest of the elements in a narrative system, the more potential there is for disruption—and for just not making sense. This is what Kay Dickinson writes about so persuasively in *Off Key: When Film and Music Won't Work Together*.

Film music anchors the image in another way as well: it positions the audience to receive the narrative in the way intended by the filmmakers. Music resonates emotion between the audience and the screen. Narrative films have developed a number of practices to assist expressive acting in portraying emotion, such as the close-up, diffuse lighting and focus, aesthetically pleasing mise-en-scène, and dialogue delivered with heightened vocal intensity. Music is the most reliable of them, harnessing the power of musical conventions to provide an audible definition of the emotion represented in the film. Elmer Bernstein puts it this way: "Music can tell the story in purely emotional terms and the film by itself cannot."

Film music does more than define emotion, however—it generates it. Samuel Chell compares music in classical Hollywood film to a television laugh track, which not only tells the audience that the show is funny but also prompts the audience to laugh at it. The pop song heard under a love scene both delineates the emotion that the onscreen characters feel and prompts the audience to identify with and share that emotion. By resonating emotion between the audience and the screen, film music engages audiences in processes of identification, which bind them into the film.

The first time we hear the song "Beauty and the Beast," it precedes any declaration of love on the part of the couple. Belle and the Beast find themselves alone together in the ballroom of the Beast's enchanted castle. Previously Belle spurned the Beast's attentions, but he has just saved her life and their icy relationship has thawed. The enchanted dinnerware and household items are doing everything they can to encourage an attachment. But no word of love is spoken. Are they or are they not falling in love? A number of cinematic elements are at work here to encourage the audience to believe that they are.

First, there is the "acting" (the look on Belle's face, the exchange of looks between the Beast and the servants) and the spectacular animation focusing on them as a couple ("camerawork," editing, and the first use of computer-generated imagery in the Disney animation canon). Then there are extratextual factors that come into play: the fairy tale on which the film is based and the audience's knowledge of other Disney animated films that end with the uniting of the couple. But the music is the crucial part of the process. The rhapsodic music exploiting conventions for passion such as violins and an upward trajectory in the melodic line, in combination with a major key, stable harmonics, and the lyrics, which voice the age-old story of romance, anchors the image to a particular meaning—that they are falling in love—while simultaneously encouraging us to participate in the couple's emotional register.

The director Lars von Trier, who actively deploys sound and music as part of his auteur signature, uses music in a diametrically opposed way; music rarely offers psychological insight into the characters or promotes emotional connections for the audience. In his Europe trilogy (1984–1991), music instead works against the characters, rendering them powerless and trapped, and even against the audience, defying conventional expectations and emotional responses, thus reinforcing von Trier's dystopic vision.

Music functions as part of an interdependent and complicated process of narrative construction in film by controlling connotation and positioning the audience to respond. This model, however, leaves some questions unanswered. Film music certainly has a narrative function, but does it always have that function? Does film music ever function nonnarratively? According to Jerrold Levinson, it does indeed. While most film music can be defined by its function in relation to narrative, some film music cannot. Levinson's litmus test is this: If the music were deleted, would the narrative content be altered in any way? If the answer is yes, then music is functioning as an element in the narrative process.

Not all film music functions in this way, according to Levinson. Some does not contribute to the construction of the narrative but functions instead as an additive, music that adds to the film but not to the narrative. An example is music that lends coherence or unity to a film, such as music that bridges a sequence to smooth over gaps in time. Music here functions not as an element in the construction of the narrative, but as an element in the construction of the film. For Levinson, music can even function both narratively and nonnarratively at the same time. While contemporary theorists agree that film music is part of a complex narrative process in film, they continue to debate a number of issues, including whether all of film music's functions are narrative.

To summarize, film music is capable of powerful effects, and those effects are the product of a unique amalgamation between two art forms. Again, film music lies at the intersection of music and film, and to understand fully how it operates we must consider both its constitution as a musical practice and its function within a cinematic practice. Music fulfills a number of important functions as an element in a film's narrative system. And it depends on the properties of music to do so.

Chapter 3
Why does film music work?

Why does film music have such power over us? What are the sources of its pleasures? And why should music have come to accompany film at all? To answer such intriguing questions, we need theory, a body of thought devoted to analyzing the deep and complex issues that underlie the framework of a discipline. Theory delves beneath the surface to get at what is neither obvious nor easily answered. Theory is always open to debate: it can be controversial and contradictory, obfuscating and illuminating, sometimes all at once. But without theory we risk becoming locked into unexamined patterns of thinking and we cannot come to terms with those fundamental questions of film music.

A lively theoretical discourse has grown up around the sources of film's powers and pleasures and the ways in which they are tied to the presence of music in film. Using the theories and methodologies of formalism, structural linguistics, narratology, reception studies, empirical studies, cognitive theory, psychoanalysis, Jungian and post-Jungian psychology, Marxism, cultural studies, feminist theory, gender studies, and queer theory, theorists of film music have investigated why music is such a potent force in film (indeed, why music is a force in films at all) and what listeners get out of listening to it. Film music theory can be covered in a variety of ways and there exists a vast array of theorical studies in film music. Here I will focus on two important theoretical and methodological responses to answering these questions: ideological analysis and psychoanalysis.

Why did music come to accompany moving images at all? Film gravitated toward music from the very beginning, both in the countries where film originated and in the countries where it arrived. The standard explanation for the amalgamation of image and music is functional: music compensated for the lack of sound in silent film, and it covered the noise produced both by the projector and by audiences unschooled in cinema etiquette. Music was readily available in the early spaces of cinema, the cafes, vaudeville theaters, music halls, carnivals, and traveling exhibitions where musicians would play for the moving images on the program as they would for live performances. But noisy projectors and audiences were soon quieted, motion pictures moved into their own screening spaces, and it was not long before synchronized sound became the norm. Yet musical accompaniment persisted in film long after its initial utility had faded. Music serves many functions in film. But understanding how film music works is not the same thing as understanding why it works. What sustained music as a practice throughout film history? What made it indispensable?

The powers of film music: ideological approaches

Theory addresses primary questions regarding the sources of film music's powers and pleasures. An investigation of these sources has led theorists in two directions: outward, toward culture where film music is produced, and inward, toward consciousness, and its many levels, where film music is perceived. The idea that music is a product of culture owes its existence to the Frankfurt school, a body of critical thought generated in and around Frankfurt, Germany, in the 1920s. Marxist critics associated with the Frankfurt school, especially Theodor Adorno and other German intellectuals such as Bertolt Brecht and Ernst Bloch, examined the contexts of economics, politics, and culture that shaped the production of art under capitalism. Attacking cherished notions of art's autonomous function, the unique creativity of the artist, and the ability of the individual to resist cultural forces, the Frankfurt school asserted that art is part of a complex and vast apparatus that largely reinforces the dominant ideological values of capitalism.

Music, like any art form, is a social discourse, structured by a set of social relations between artist and perceiver. For Adorno, music has a unique position among the arts. Because it seems more direct and less mediated by culture, music has the most power to serve a political function under capitalism: to pacify dangerous, anarchic impulses by lulling listeners into an acceptance of the status quo, distracting them from the alienating effects of life under capitalism. He is especially hard on popular music, "a training course in . . . passivity."

Adorno, in collaboration with composer Hanns Eisler, extended this argument to film music in *Composing for the Films*. Music binds the spectator into the film and masks the film's material constitution as a technological product. Film music for Adorno and Eisler is "a cement, which holds together elements that otherwise would oppose each other unrelated—the mechanical product and the spectators." Film music's adhesion stems from its exceptional ability to create and resonate emotion between the screen and the spectator. In so doing, film music distracts spectators from film's materiality. Thus film music fulfills a potent ideological function: to promote an audience's absorption into the film and thus position that audience to accept, uncritically, the cultural values circulating through a film. It is not without significance that Adorno and Eisler refer to film music as a drug. That art serves a political function was a radical notion in postwar America. Adorno's authorship of *Composing for the Films* was suppressed in English-language editions, and Eisler, an émigré who had found work composing in Hollywood, was summoned before the House Un-American Activities Committee and forced to leave the United States. That art is inextricably tied to politics seems painfully obvious in Eisler's case.

The ideological analysis of film music has been taken up by many film scholars. In Claudia Gorbman's groundbreaking *Unheard Melodies: Narrative Film Music*, Gorbman opens up Adorno and Eisler's insights by comparing film music to easy-listening music, or what is often called elevator music. The similarities are illuminating. Both operate as part of a larger field of reference, whether a literal elevator, a shopping mall, a dentist's office, or narrative film, and both are regulated by a larger context that determines its presence or absence, the interruption of a mall's background music to make announcements, or the decreased volume of the film score under dialogue.

Neither elevator music nor film music draws attention to itself or demands the listener's full attention and both drive away unpleasantness, whether it be drilling in the dentist's office or the technological basis of cinema. Music encourages us to consume the products of culture and makes consumption easy, whether the product is material, such as the goods on display at the mall, or immaterial, such as film images. Ultimately, Gorbman theorizes, film music lulls "the spectator into becoming an *untroublesome* (less critical, less wary) *viewing subject*." Film music makes us more likely to brush away doubts about what the film might be promoting, to suspend our disbelief in the two-dimensional, larger-than-life images posing as reality, and ultimately to accept, uncritically, a series of images and the cultural values they encode.

Similarly intrigued by music's ideological function in film, Caryl Flinn theorizes that one of the most potent discourses attached to music is a utopian discourse: music's ability to offer "an impression of perfection and integrity in an otherwise imperfect and unintegrated world." Music offers listeners a "fullness of experience…an ability to return…to better, allegedly more 'perfect' times and memories." Film scores transport listeners from the technological and fragmented experience of a postindustrial capitalism and its mechanically reproduced art forms to an idealized past of wholeness. According to Flinn's argument, film music always carries with it traces of plenitude, wrapping film content in a kind of nostalgia and making us desire what the film offers. In the process we become less critical of a film's values and value judgments.

Theory can seem exceedingly abstract but its application can have profound consequences for our understanding of film. The manner in which cultural ideology manifests itself through music is neither direct, because much of its operation takes place on less than a conscious plane, nor immediately obvious; it is complex, sometimes contradictory, and elusive. The results of that process, however, are clearly audible. When in a Hollywood film noir you hear a bluesy saxophone in accompaniment to a woman, what do you assume about her sexuality? What difference would it make to hear a lush romantic cue featuring a sweet violin instead?

Starting in the 1980s, feminist scholars were drawn to Hollywood film noir, delineating the musical stereotypes that Hollywood composers drew on to represent female sexuality. These clichéd conventions (saxophones and bluesy performance practices for women whose sexuality operated outside social norms; violins in upward trajectories for virtuous girlfriends, wives, and especially mothers) encoded a set of responses and value judgments consistent with dominant cultural values about female sexuality. Take a listen to the score for *Blade Runner* (1982) and its iconic use of the saxophone to hear for yourself.

The ideological function of film music has been a particularly rich site of investigation into how history, gender, sexuality, race, class, and ethnicity are encoded in a film's score. Some classic examples of the diverse body of scholarship in this area—and this is a short list limited to book-length monographs—include Krin Gabbard's analysis of how jazz encodes cultural ideologies about race and sexuality; Anahid Kassabian's study of the impact of song choice on the representation of gender in contemporary Hollywood film; and Caryl Flinn's study of music and the relationship between history, culture, and ideology in New German film.

Since the publication of the first edition of this book in 2010, the number of studies that employ ideological analysis to examine fundamental questions of film music has continued to grow, particularly studies of gender and sexuality in relation to cultural ideologies. In 2012, *Music, Sound, and the Moving Image* dedicated a special issue to the subject. And in 2017, the anthology *Spectatorship: Shifting Theories of Gender, Sexuality, and the Media* appeared. Recent examples of feminist scholarship include articles by Catherine Haworth on music in the female gothic film; Zhichun Lin on a cross-cultural analysis of theme music and femininity in Hollywood and Chinese versions of *Letter from an Unknown Woman*; Laura Miranda on gendered constructions in Francoist Spanish film; and monographs by Peter Franklin on gender in Romanticism and modernism, Heather Laing on the gendered score in melodrama and the woman's film, and Amanda Howell on masculinity in the contemporary pop score.

Queer theorists have investigated along similar lines, unpacking musical representations for nonheteronormative sexuality in relation to cultural hierarchies. Recent examples include articles by Todd Decker on musical closeting of homosexual characters in *The Talented Mr. Ripley*; Catherine Howard on encoding homosexuality through musical signifiers for the femme fatale; Miguel Mera on outing the score, examining scoring approaches that challenge traditional musical modes of sexual representation; Susanna Välimäki on the audiovisual construction of transgender identity in *Transamerica*; and the monograph by Jack Curtis Dubowsky on film, music, and queerness.

The pleasures of film music: psychoanalysis

Film music is produced through culture, but it is perceived by individuals. Some film music is perceived consciously: we would not come out of a film remembering its music or be induced to buy a soundtrack recording otherwise. But if we are to analyze fully film music's power and understand the pleasures it offers us, we need to address how film music works in another register: the unconscious. Watching film is enjoyable. It has a unique hold over us, an ability to make us forget where we are or who we are when we are engrossed in watching it. Psychoanalysis, a theory of the mind that seeks to understand the operation of the unconscious, can help us grasp why this hypnotic fascination is so pleasurable and specifically what part music plays in this fascination.

Beginning in the 1970s and 1980s, French and North American theorists turned to psychoanalysis to bring music into focus. Music plays a key role in human psychic development. From our earliest moments inside the womb, we experience the elements of music: the rhythmic patterns of our mother's heartbeat, breathing, and pulse as well as the pitch and dynamics of her voice. In fact, the womb is often described in psychoanalysis in acoustic terms as a "sonorous envelope of the self," in the words of Didier Anzieu, the "sonorous space" of Gerard Blanchard, or "the murmuring house" of Guy Rosolato.

We know, for instance, that a newborn can already recognize its mother's voice. After birth, the infant continues in a bath of aural stimulation, including and especially the mother's voice, which, again, is experienced as music. (Think of the ways in which language itself incorporates musical elements such as rhythm, pitch, dynamics, and intonation and the musical way we talk to babies.)

Psychoanalysis posits the pleasure of music as stemming from both our prebirth experience and our earliest, prelinguistic existence. Music allows us to experience what we are forced to repress in our adult lives: longings for a return to the original state of plentitude and fusion with the mother, a fusion we experienced as music. Rosolato argues that Western harmony, with its patterns of divergence and unity, can be understood psychoanalytically as the "dramatization of these separated and reunited bodies" of mother and child. But it is not only Western music that can claim a connection between its music and elemental psychic processes.

Why does film music work?

The famed *taiko* drummer Daihaichi Oguchi explained the lure of the taiko drum in similar terms: "Your heart is a taiko. All people listen to a taiko rhythm *'dontsuku-dontsuku'* in their mother's womb."

Psychoanalysis helps to account for music's centrality in human experience. Music stimulates us to regress back to that complete sense of satisfaction and pleasure that the union with the mother represents. When we watch films and hear film music, something similar happens. A number of factors, the comfortable seats, the darkened auditorium, the hypnotic effect of the bright images on the screen, and the music come together to encourage us to regress back to a psychic state of profound plenitude and satisfaction. This is what gives film music such a powerful hold over us and at least partially explains why it is in film at all. Film music short-circuits consciousness, as Gorbman points out, "bypassing the usual censors of the preconscious," facilitating the hypnotic power of film and encouraging us to regress to a place of complete psychic satisfaction. No wonder we love going to the movies!

Psychoanalytically informed theories of film music have come under fire from cognitive theorists who argue that psychoanalysis ignores the conscious work performed by audiences as they experience a film. Pointing to the successful soundtrack recording industry, the popularity of songs conceived for films, and the millions of film music fans around the world, among other reasons, cognitivists posit that we interpret music in the same way that we do any other cinematic element: by processing the information it presents us. For example, Ben Winters argues that it is our active engagement with musical conventions that allows us to simulate the emotions experienced by on-screen characters and share in their response, a process he describes as "far from subliminal." Jeff Smith has written the most sustained cognitivist critique of psychoanalytic film music theory by posing a series of difficult questions, among them: How does psychoanalysis account for the intermittence of film music? Since film music, in sound film at least, is not a continuous but a fragmentary phenomenon, how are the unconscious processes it activates sustained when it is absent? What is the relationship between the unconscious and conscious perception of film music? How much or what part of music is unheard? Cognitive film theorists argue that a psychoanalytic theory of film music is not yet fully realized and needs to take into account a number of unresolved issues. But if we are looking for the sources of our fascination with film music and our pleasures in listening to it, we should not dismiss the relationship between music and the unconscious.

Film music theorists have offered thought-provoking ideas about the sources of music's powers and pleasures. Their work has prompted deep and far-reaching reflections on both the nature of power itself, how it circulates through culture and is manifested through its art forms, and the power of the unconscious, which underlies all of human activity. Theory should do no less.

Chapter 4
A history of film music I: 1895–1927

Film music originated and developed in the era known paradoxically as silent film. Outlining this history, which stretches from the inauguration of moving pictures to the widespread adoption of synchronized sound, is beset with problems: evidence is scant or nonexistent (much is lost or was not written down in the first place); primary source materials are scattered in libraries and archives around the globe; overgeneralizations and misconceptions promulgated by the earliest film histories continue to haunt the field; and a focus on the United States has given it an outsize role in this history. All of these conditions have made it difficult to document fully the history of film music and especially its global practice. Still, scholars of film music in this earliest period are recovering more and more of this history. (There is now even an online website devoted to the collection and dissemination of the materials of silent film accompaniment.) Thus, it is possible at least to trace out the main lines of film music's development from its inception to the advent of sound film.

Music and the origins of motion pictures

"The idea occurred to me that it was possible to devise an instrument which should do for the eye what the phonograph does for the ear," Thomas Edison famously wrote. But it is his description of what he imagined that instrument could do that underscores the primacy of music in Edison's enterprise. "My intention is to have such a happy combination of electricity and photography that a man can sit in his own parlor and see reproduced on a screen…the players in an opera…, and…he will hear the sound of their voices as they talk or sing or laugh." Although Edison never realized his visionary concept of audiovisual home entertainment, music was to prove central to the history of motion pictures.

One early effort at synchronized sound at the Edison laboratories has survived in an experimental film made around 1894–95 by W. K. L. Dickson, head of Edison's motion picture division, known as the *Dickson Experimental Sound Film*. Two male employees dance to music from Robert Planquette's 1877 opera, *The Chimes of Normandy*, played by Dickson himself on the violin into the phonograph horn visible in the frame. It is the only known surviving example of a synchronized sound film at Edison. Dickson's performance is often cited as the first example of musical accompaniment, but that description does not do justice to the driving force of music here. In some sense, it is the images that accompany the music, more like a forerunner of today's music videos. And, while Dickson's film may well have been a step toward Edison's dream of opera in the home, its music could well point in another direction, to the centrality of popular music in early film accompaniment. "Song of the Cabin Boy," the piece Dickson played, may be derived from a high art source, but it was repackaged as a popular song and marketed for mass consumption by the time Dickson played it, an early example of crossover music. Dickson's experiment was not repeated and the synchronization of image and sound at Edison stalled.

The quest for musical accompaniment, however, did not. The Edison company was banking on the Kinetoscope, a peep-show device that presented silent moving images to a single spectator. Within a year of its public debut in 1894, the Kinetoscope was modified, with the addition of a phonograph and ear tubes, into a Kinetophone to present Edison films—musical performances of one sort or another—with musical accompaniment, specifically chosen phonograph recordings from the Edison catalog. Image and sound were not synchronized; rather the music was chosen to loosely fit the images. What evidence there is (and it is scant) suggests that popular dance tunes and marches were used in these matchups: "La Paloma" for *Carmencita* (1894); Irish jigs for *Lucy Murray* (1894) and *May Lucas* (1894); "Tobasco" for *Annabel Serpentine Dance* (1894). Kinetophones found their way as far afield as Nizhniy Novgorod, Russia. But the Kinetophone was short-lived and soon replaced by projected images for communal audiences. Films now screened in entertainment venues such as vaudeville, carnivals, and burlesque, where musicians played for the moving images as they did for the live performers.

Music accompanied the first motion pictures in Europe. In France and Germany early films were projected onto large screens and shown to communal audiences. These screenings were accompanied by music—or soon would be. But these screenings used live music. In 1892 in Paris, Émile Reynaud showed *Pantomimes lumineuses*, a series of animated projections, to music composed for the occasion by Gaston Paulin. In December 1895, the Lumière brothers would famously introduce their *cinématographe* to the public; Emile Maraval played the piano that night. In November 1895, Max Skladanowsky in Berlin, who beat the Lumières to the punch by almost two months, presented films of acrobats, dancers, boxers, and animal acts. Skladanowsky used a combination of original compositions and preexisting music performed live, an intriguing mix of polkas, gallops, waltzes, and marches. A selection from Mikhail Glinka's symphonic poem *Kamarinskaya* is supposed to have accompanied the Russian dancers.

The first screenings of the *cinématographe* in Great Britain took place in London music halls in 1896. Newspaper accounts indicate that theater orchestras provided music. At the first screening of film in the Netherlands, the percussionist in the theater orchestra played a drum roll to accompany a moving train, perhaps the Lumieres' *Arrival of the Train at the Station* (1895).

As film wended its way around the world, music followed. It is as if film exerted a gravitational pull on music, no matter where films were screened. Live and recorded music materialized at screenings across six continents.

Although some of the first histories of early film exhibition assumed accompaniment was live, early on it was often heard in recorded form. Phonograph recordings were often used to lure audiences for whom hearing the phonograph might have been as novel an experience as seeing moving images. In the Czech territories, the first moving images were accompanied by phonograph recordings. In Berlin, Oskar Messter used them to accompany films. In Prague, phonographs were equipped with oversized horns so they could be heard throughout an auditorium. Within a few short years, phonograph recordings were ubiquitous across Europe, and by 1903 a cinema in Brussels was devoted exclusively to phonographic sound, showcasing short films of operatic performances. As late as 1929 Luis Buñuel and Salvatore Dali's avant-garde film, *Un chien andalou*, was accompanied in Paris by phonograph records of Argentine tangos and Wagnerian opera. There are accounts of phonographic accompaniment in Poland, Australia, and Mexico. In Iran, phonographic accompaniment had a particularly long history, lasting through the 1920s.

Phonograph recordings were an important feature of early film exhibition in the United States too, where they were used through the nickelodeon era, ca. 1905–7. Converted storefronts in urban neighborhoods dedicated to screening films, nickelodeons presented a varied program of moving pictures, variety acts, illustrated songs (slides with illustrations and lyrics so the audiences could sing along), and musical performances with various forms of musical accompaniment including phonograph recordings. Often the phonograph would be positioned outside the nickelodeon, doing double duty as ballyhoo to lure passersby and as accompaniment for the show inside.

Musical accompaniment and women

Female musicians functioning as accompanists, conductors, musical directors, cue sheet creators, and even composers were an integral part of cinema-going across the era in many parts of the world. All-female orchestras such as the Pavilion Ladies' Orchestra in Dublin, the Fadettes of Boston [Orchestra], and the Evington Cinema Orchestra in Leicester lent respectability to an entertainment finding its foothold. Vitagraph star John Bunny, on location in Ireland, is said to have remarked upon hearing the Ladies' Irish Orchestra, "An orchestra composed of women is an undeniable asset."

Women's roles in accompaniment expanded during World War I when male musicians left for military service. The phenomenon of women musicians was relatively short-lived in Ireland. When cinema's credentials as a refined form of entertainment were established, female orchestras were replaced, often by male concert musicians supplementing their income. In Britain, women were expected to give up their jobs to returning veterans. And discrimination abounded, especially in terms of pay. Women soldiered on until the coming of sound, which ended the careers of female and male cinema musicians alike.

Although research on women as directors, screenwriters, editors, cinematographers, producers, production chiefs, and exhibitors has transformed the history of early film, research on the roles that women played in the musical life of early cinema has lagged behind. Recent scholarship by Denis Condon, Kendra Preston Leonard, and Laraine Porter has brought to light the role of women in musical accompaniment in Ireland, the United States, and Great Britain. Much work, however, remains to be done.

1. Rosa Rio at the Wurlitzer organ at Brooklyn's Fox Theater. Many women served as accompanists in the silent era. Rio's career was especially noteworthy. When sound film replaced live musicians, Rio worked in the radio, recording, and television industries and continued to accompany silent films in live performances. She also provided the accompaniment for more than 350 videotapes of silent films.

Musical accompaniment: What music? Whose music?

In the first decade of film history, music proved central to the experience of film around the world. But different film traditions in various countries devised different approaches to musical accompaniment. In the United States and Western Europe, popular music was heard alongside concert music. In many national cinemas, however, accompanists gravitated toward indigenous music, both traditional and popular. In Russia, for instance, many accompanists depended on native Russian music and often paid no attention to the image track as they performed it. Russian audiences, it appears, were not dismayed. In Ireland, it was popular Irish tunes and songs that accompanists depended on. Musical accompaniment could function as a powerful medium of cultural dissemination, and it would play an increasingly important role in this capacity as the silent period progressed.

In India, Lumières '*cinématographe* was shown in Bombay (now Mumbai) in July 1896. It is likely that the earliest screenings were silent. Given the strong tradition of indigenous song and dance in Indian theater, it is not surprising that live musical accompaniment quickly found its way into Indian cinemas, reported as early as August 1896 by *Times of India*. Traditionally, English films would be screened with popular Western songs played on Western instruments, while locally produced Indian films would be accompanied by classical rāgas and folk songs played on traditional Indian instruments such as the tabla (drum), the sarangi (bowed lute), and the harmonium, adapted for use in India with drone stops. There is evidence, however, that these two traditions sometimes intersected: violins and clarinets were heard along with Indian instruments during Indian films, and the sarangi was heard with Western instruments during English films.

In Iran, the first films may have been the home movies made of the Shah's European trip in 1900. Soon motion pictures became a leisure activity of royalty and the upper class. When the first public cinema opened in Tehran in 1904, films screened there were virtually all foreign, imported from the West, and lecturer-translators could be heard along with live musical accompaniment utilizing Western music and instruments, often piano and violin, or phonograph recordings from the West. Theaters would also position musicians at the entrance to provide ballyhoo to passersby before moving into the theater (and behind the screen) to accompany the films. As cinema-going developed in Iran, theaters drawing on lower-class audiences opened, but here indigenous Persian music played before, during, and after films.

In Japan, the Kinetoscope, Vitascope, and *cinématographe* had all arrived by 1897. Early on, exhibitors used bands playing on barges near viewing spaces to advertise the screenings and provide background music for them. Soon, musical accompaniment was performed by small orchestras positioned behind the audience. The subject matter of many of the earliest Japanese-produced films centered around music. In 1899 in Tokyo, films of geisha dancers were presented on the bill in variety show theaters where it is highly probable that the musicians in the pit orchestra provided some form of musical accompaniment. By 1908 some theaters employed a full orchestra and live singers for film screenings.

In Japan, as in India, musical accompaniment to screenings of foreign films utilized Western instruments and melodies, often derived from opera. Accompaniment for films produced in Japan, however, utilized traditional Japanese music and instruments such as the shamisen (three-stringed banjo) and taiko drums. Evidence suggests that in practice, however, musical accompaniment was sometimes a hybrid of the two practices, mixing traditional Japanese and Western musical elements during performances of both foreign and locally produced films.

In China and Hong Kong, music similarly proved central to the experience of film. In Shanghai, the first films were shown in 1896. Edison's Vitascope debuted in May 1897; by July of that year the local newspaper noted live piano accompaniment. The first indigenously produced films in Peking (now Beijing), *Dingjun Mountain* (1905), and in Hong Kong, *Stealing a Roast Duck* (1909), were of performances drawn from famous Chinese operas. *Dingjun Mountain* was supposedly shot with live music on the set, and it seems likely that selections from the operatic source were reproduced by local musicians on native instruments when the film was screened.

The earliest indigenous Brazilian films have not survived, but their titles, such as *Dance of a Bahian* (1899) and *Capoeira Dance* (1905), allude to Bahia, an Afro-Brazilian community, and the music produced there. Again, it is hard to imagine that these dance films were shown without some attempt at re-creating Afro-Brazilian music such as the samba. Brazilian filmmakers mined Brazilian popular music and musical performers throughout the silent era.

Vocal accompaniment was also a part of early film exhibition, both spoken (lecturers who interpreted films for the audience) and sung (singers positioned behind or next to the screen). Lecturers were an especially important part of the filmgoing experience in Japan, Korea, Taiwan, and Japanese American communities in California. Called benshi in Japan, these lecturers were so important that musicians providing accompaniment deferred to them by stopping the music when the benshi spoke.

Lecturers could serve a dual function as accompanists too. In India, singers lectured in song form. Vocal accompaniment blossomed with the rise of feature film with soloists and choruses joining orchestras. In Ireland, Brian MacGowan, star of *Knocknagow* (1918), toured with the film, appearing on stage to sing his songs synchronized to his on-screen performance. In the Netherlands, opera singers appearing in *Gloria Transita* (1918) sang the quartet from *Rigoletto* along with the film at some performances. New research by Klaus Tieber and Anna K. Windisch reveals that in Vienna, a kind of rough synchronization between film and performer was attempted in filmed operas like *Martha* (1914, remade 1918). Singers were hidden in the orchestra pit and, through a complex system of synchronization involving mirrors, could synchronize their voices to the film, fostering the illusion that the on-screen singers were producing the sound.

Some films, however, screened in silence. While the earliest histories of the period posited that film was never silent, with the venue always filled with some kind of musical accompaniment, Rick Altman has shown otherwise. His groundbreaking research reveals that silence, although not typical, did fill screening venues across the United States. Altman even makes the case that the first screenings of Edison's projected films at Koster & Bial's Music Hall in New York did not use the music described in newspaper accounts to accompany the films, but to provide fanfare to introduce them. (He also suggests the same for Emile Maraval's piano performance at the Lumieres' first screening.) In Russia it took more than a decade for musical accompaniment in any form to assert itself and some films, perhaps even into the 1910s, screened in silence.

Music and moving image existed in a complex relationship in the first decade of film history. Some films screened in silence, but most films were accompanied by music of some kind. Some music was provided by phonograph recordings, but most was live. Live accompaniment could mean a single musician, often a pianist, a small ensemble of players, or a theater orchestra sometimes joined by vocalists. Some musical accompaniment was intermittent, some was continuous. Some accompaniment was improvised, and that improvisation may or may not have responded to the events on screen. Some accompaniment was originally composed for a specific film even in this early period, but most accompaniment depended on preexisting music. Indigenous music, both traditional and contemporary, proved a staple throughout the world. This diversity underscores the fact that the earliest examples of musical accompaniment did not reflect a single, unifying practice.

Musical accompaniment: the birth of an art form

Beginning around 1906 and continuing through the 1910s, the film business was characterized by efforts to stabilize the fledging industry as a profitable enterprise and establish its legitimacy as an art form. These efforts included the development of a narrative-based medium (such as the classical narrative tradition in the United States) and the expansion of film length (ultimately culminating in the 60- to 120-minute feature-length film); the evolution and standardization of film technology and the development of techniques to facilitate a narrative-based medium; the upgrading of film content (such as the adaptations of literary and stage classics by the *Film d'Art* company in France or the filming of Kabuki troupes in Japan); the gentrification of viewing spaces evolving into the elaborate picture palaces of the 1910s and 1920s; and the attraction of larger audiences. Musical accompaniment was a critical part of this transformation. Attempts to encourage the appropriate and continuous presence of live accompaniment and to police its quality originated at this time. It would not be long before the quality of musical accompaniment would be a factor that exhibitors touted to market their theaters.

A number of institutions and practices fostered this transformation. Trade publications addressed music, disseminating techniques, setting standards, and advocating the live and continuous presence of music. In France, Gaumont began circulating a weekly *Guide Musicale* to exhibitors as early as 1907, and in the United States, "Incidental Music for Edison Pictures" appeared in the *Edison Kinetograms* beginning in 1909. Other studios, trade publications, and entrepreneurs also began making suggestions for suitable types of music. Evolving throughout the 1910s, the cue sheet (as it came to be known) was a list of musical pieces designed to help accompanists create a seamless and appropriate score. In the United States, selections culled from a variety of sources including standards of the concert hall, especially nineteenth-century concert and operatic music, folk tunes, popular music, and original compositions, were cued to specific moments in a film. Later, cue sheets derived from original scores were circulated in locations where orchestral resources were limited, a reminder that throughout the silent era, the same film could be heard with different music depending on where it screened.

Cue sheets often circulated with films as they traversed the globe. On the one hand, films produced in the United States typically were exported with cue sheets, and in China, newspapers report that accompanists used them for screenings. In Vienna, on the other hand, a city with a long musical heritage, such imported cue sheets were largely ignored and musicians created their own accompaniments. Irish films produced for export to the United States circulated with cue sheets of Irish popular music. As cue sheets evolved, they became more elaborate, including excerpts from musical selections, timings, and intricate directions for coordinating music and image. Cue sheets depended on the numerous musical encyclopedias, which began to be published at roughly the same time.

Musical encyclopedias contained inventories of music, some originally composed for use in the cinema and some preexisting, cataloged by their narrative utility. Among the most influential were Giuseppi Becce's *Kinothek* series published in Berlin (1919–29) and J. S. Zamecnik's *Sam Fox Moving Picture Music* series (1913–23) and Erno Rapee's *Motion Picture Moods for Pianists and Organists* (1924) published in the United States. These encyclopedias extensively cataloged narrative situations accompanists might face and suggested appropriate music. Zamecnik's "Indian Music," for instance, provides an all-purpose cue for the presence of American Indians on screen. Zamecnik's "Hurry Music" was customized for struggles, duels, and mob or fire scenes. Even treachery was adapted for villains, ruffians, smugglers, or conspirators. Rapee's *Encyclopedia* had dozens of categories, offering music from battles to weddings (and almost everything in between). Musical encyclopedias in one form or another were used worldwide. In Japan, accompanists were provided with catalogs of mood music; in Russia, Anatoli Goldobin and Boris Azancheyev published *Accompanying Cinematograph Pictures on the Piano* in 1912.

Much of the music of the silent era, though, was ephemeral, not written down, or, if it was, not intended to be saved. And it was not recorded. The result is that much of what we know about the form and character of musical accompaniment comes from the surviving discourses surrounding early film music: cue sheets, encyclopedias, advice columns in trade publications, newspaper reviews, how-to manuals, and oral histories. These sources help us to reconstruct how music sounded and functioned in the era. Unfortunately, these resources are scattered in libraries and archives around the globe. Access is limited. There is much work left to be done uncovering these resources to have a complete picture of music in this era.

INDIAN MUSIC

2. "Indian Music" from J. S. Zamecnick's *Moving Picture Music*, Vol. 1 (1913). "Indian music" is typical of the generic approach of musical collections in this era, with the tom-tom rhythm in the bass clef derived from stereotypes about Indians, not actual Native American music.

From extant sources, we can see that by the 1910s, in the United States and Europe, film music had gravitated toward providing a few functions: identifying geographic location and period, intensifying mood, delineating emotion, illustrating onscreen action, and fleshing out characterization. Accompanists came to rely on musical conventions (some might say clichés) to do so, such as tremolo for suspense, pizzicato for sneakiness, and dissonance for villainy. In fact, mood music became so central to silent film accompaniment that it was often played on the set to motivate the actors during filming.

As musical accompaniment began to coalesce around these functions, the use of popular music was beginning to chafe against them. Popular music served a key role in silent film exhibition. Publications on musical accompaniment in the United States and western Europe, however, were beginning to advocate limiting its use and decried the practice of selecting popular songs based on the appropriateness of their titles. Some influential musical directors at large urban movie theaters even tried to rid cinema of popular music. In New York, Erno Rapee, an eminent film music composer and conductor and the author of two important encyclopedias of film music, frequently complained about the audience's preference for popular music. Rapee made it a personal crusade to replace popular music with concert music but he was not entirely successful in doing so. Hollywood saw the handwriting on the wall, and by the 1920s many studios began promoting songs composed expressly for their films and buying music publishing houses to market them.

Studies on the impact of race and ethnicity on film reception similarly underscore the centrality of popular music and the trouble it could cause. Mary Carbine's research has shown that in Chicago's African American community, where Fats Waller and Louis Armstrong once played in movie theater orchestras, blues and jazz accompanied screenings for Black audiences of films produced for white audiences. Armstrong noted how the musicians ignored what was transpiring on screen to concentrate on their playing, a practice that generated complaints from some audience members who found such unmotivated accompaniment distracting. Popular music during this era—its various practices and the discourses surrounding it—reminds us that musical accompaniment could function transgressively and thus become a potential site of cultural struggle.

It is interesting to speculate on how much of this transgressive potential was tapped in other places. As we have seen, in many countries where national cinemas developed, indigenous popular musics were incorporated into filmic accompaniment for films produced locally. Here music becomes an expressive gesture toward national identity. But indigenous music was also incorporated into the accompaniment of foreign films imported to Ireland, India, Iran, Russia, Turkey, and Japan and perhaps many other places. I am reminded of the early Japanese film entrepreneur Toyojiro Takamatsu, who traveled around Japan screening films. For the foreign films, Takamatsu provided voice-over mistranslation, transforming films, no matter what their original content, into examples of his own socialist politics. Did music aid and abet his politics?

Hamid Naficy posits that the Persian music utilized in Iranian theaters "both indigenized and deconstructed the foreign films." Savaş Arslan argues along similar lines for Turkish films, describing the military bands that played for screenings of Western films as "a specific domestic, nationalistic intervention." And screenings of US films in the Dutch East Indies (now Indonesia) were described as having "satirical musical accompaniment."

We need more research to flesh out exactly what happened when indigenous music was heard during screenings. To what extent did such music transform or critique film content? Music mediates the reception of films and can challenge the technologies, values, and narratives tied up in them. The power of music as a point of cultural interface in early film exhibition, indeed a potential site of resistance, is an area of film music scholarship that needs to expand.

Film scores commissioned for specific films began to emerge in the first decade of the twentieth century. Although examples existed as early as the 1890s, the phenomenon was given cultural legitimacy by the French Film d'Art company, which yoked prestige productions to scores by prominent concert hall composers, such as Camille Saint-Saëns's for *L'Assassinat du Duc de Guise* (1908). In Russia Mikhail Ippolitov-Ivanov scored *Stenka Razin* (1908), and in Italy Pietro Mascagni scored *Satan's Rhapsody* (1915). By the 1920s Erik Satie, Darius Milhaud, Arthur Honegger, George Antheil, and Dmitri Shostakovich had all written film scores. Richard Strauss scored the film version of his opera *Der Rosenkavalier* (1926) and conducted the orchestra at the premiere.

Not all scores commissioned for individual films, however, are original in the way we might suppose them to be. Rather, some are compilations, cobbled together from a variety of sources and sometimes including original composition. Martin Marks's pioneering research on the Joseph Breil and D. W. Griffith score for *The Birth of a Nation* (1915) reveals that while the score is original to that film, it is a compilation of such symphonic chestnuts as Richard Wagner's "Ride of the Valkyries" and Edvard Grieg's "In the Hall of the Mountain King," as well as patriotic tunes, popular songs, minstrel music, and some new composition, notably a love theme supposedly penned by Griffith himself.

Richard Wagner exerted an influence on film accompanists from the beginning. His theory of the *gesamtkunstwerk* (total art work) provided a model for the ways in which music could be attentive to the drama, and his use of the leitmotif became a model for unifying the accompaniment and clarifying the story. As early as

1910, a cue sheet for the Edison company's *Frankenstein* uses a theme from Carl Maria von Weber's opera *Der Freischütz* as a leitmotif for the monster. In the same year, *Moving Picture News* reported that the use of the leitmotif is a "natural law that must on no account be broken." Russian newspapers reported that the "melodic themes" accompanying *The Terrible Vengeance* (1913) "fitted the characters perfectly." Still, the Wagnerian leitmotif was not universally adopted and some high-profile composers abandoned it, among them Shostakovich, Antheil, and Satie. By the 1920s, audiences in many parts of the world could expect a preplanned, largely nonimprovisatory, continuous musical accompaniment responding in some way to screen content and performed at a certain level of expertise.

The piano may have been the workhorse of the era, but the theater organ was the star. The Mighty Wurlitzer, developed specifically for film accompaniment, was the gold standard in the United States, with numerous theatrical stops to create sound effects.

3. The Capitol was one of New York's premier movie theaters, and it boasted first-class orchestral accompaniment. Here, David Mendoza conducts the Capitol Grand Orchestra. Note organ in foreground.

One of its many competitors, the Morton pipe organ, boasted a telephone ring, door knocks, church and sleigh bells, steamboat, train, police and bird whistles, car horns, fire gongs, surf, wind, thunder, horse hooves, airplane motors, castanets, and Chinese gongs. In large cities, motion picture orchestras provided accompaniment in palatial theaters built exclusively for film. The Roxy Theater in New York boasted an orchestra of more than one hundred players. Some conductors even rivaled a film's director in name recognition.

The apex of the silent film score

The 1920s witnessed the great flowering of the film score. Music was specifically created for many films of the late silent era, which extended in some parts of the world into the 1930s: *Nosferatu* (1922), scored by Hans Erdmann; *Metropolis* (1927), scored by Gottfried Huppertz; *La Roue* (1923), scored by Arthur Honegger; *Broken Blossoms* (1919), scored by Louis F. Gottschalk; and *The Thief of Bagdad* (1924), scored by Mortimer Wilson. Cutting-edge composition and scoring techniques could be heard in Shostakovich's score for *The New Babylon* (1929), where music, including a wonderfully demented can-can that starts to deconstruct before our very ears, undercuts the image track as often as it supports it; in Edmund Meisel's modernist score for *Battleship Potemkin* (1925), blamed for causing riots at the Berlin premiere and banned in Germany; in Antheil's dissonant score for *Ballet mécanique* (1924); and in Satie's score for the Dada film *Entr'acte* (1924), conceived as part of an evening of anarchy. In Argentina, screenings of *La muchacha del arrabal* (1922) were accompanied by tangos, with lyrics penned by the film's director, José Ferreyra. In Iran, the director Ebrahim Moradi composed the score for *Bolhavas* (1933) himself.

Silent films continue to be rescued from oblivion and music has become a key part of this process. In the early twenty-first century, silent film with musical accompaniment can be experienced in a variety of formats. The most exciting is the presentation of silent film with live musical accompaniment at film festivals, museums, and archives, in opera houses and concert halls, and sometimes even in the very places where they were first heard, film theaters. Inaugurated in the 1970s, the phenomenon is exemplified in the work of scholar/conductor Gillian Anderson, who for decades now has been recovering, reconstructing, and conducting original film scores for silent films.

In the 1980s live orchestral accompaniment to silent film went into high gear: *Napoleon* (1927) in London in 1980 screened with a new score by Carl Davis and in New York in 1981 with a different new score by Carmine Coppola; and *The New Babylon* (1929) in 1983 with its original score by Shostakovich. The Silent Film Festival at Pordenone, Italy, has been presenting live musical accompaniment to all its screenings since 1982. As silent films have been restored and/or reconstructed, musical scores have come to the fore. Some restorations/reconstructions use the original scores, such as those for *Battleship Potemkin*, *Nosferatu*, and *Metropolis*. Some use scores that aim for authenticity, composed in the historical style of the era, such as Robert Israel's scores for *The Cheat* (1915), *Kino-eye* (1922), and *La Roue* (1923) or the Alloy Orchestra's score for *The Man with the Movie Camera* (1929), based on the music notes of its director, Dziga Vertov.

A lively new art form has developed alongside these: contemporary scores for silent films from a wide array of musical styles, modalities, and artists, some performed live and some recorded for the soundtrack of reconstructions/restorations. There is jazz trombonist Wycliffe Gordon's jazz score for *Body and Soul* (1925); Giorgio Moroder's disco score for *Metropolis*; the Pet Shop Boys' synth score for *Battleship Potemkin*; Damien Coldwell's bluegrass score for *Tol'able David* (1921); Pixies' frontman Black Francis's rock score for *The Golem* (1920); KTL's electroacoustic score for *The Phantom Carriage* (1921); and Yat-Kha's mix of traditional Mongolian music (including Tuvan throat singing, no less!) and Western pop/rock for *Storm over Asia* (1928). Some commercial reconstructions/restorations even offer multiple scores (original, historically based, and contemporary) for the same film, such as Kino Lorber's *Sherlock Jr.* (1924). Sadly, a performance of a live score can be a one-off (like Yat-Kha's for *Storm over Asia*) or run into production problems as a recorded soundtrack (like the Pet Shop Boys' score for *Battleship Potemkin*), not to mention the fact that existing reconstructions/restorations go out of "print" far too often. There is always eBay.

With the advent of the twenty-first century, an exciting new field of scholarship has developed around the contemporary score for silent film, including three recent books: K. J. Donnelly and Ann-Kristin Wallengren's anthology, *Today's Sounds for Yesterday's Films*; Ruth Barton and Simon Trezise's anthology, *Music and Sound in the Silent Film: From the Nickelodeon to* The Artist; and Phillip Johnston's monograph, *Silent Films/Loud Music: New Ways of Listening to and Thinking About Silent Film Music*.

Chapter 5
A history of film music II: 1927–1970

The quest for synchronization and its realization long preceded the worldwide conversion to sound. W. K. L. Dickson at Edison achieved a rough synchronization of music and image as early as 1894/95. Oskar Messter in Germany, Léon Gaumont in France, Cecil Hepworth in England, and Kazimierz Proszynski in Poland devised sound systems for large-screen projection, all of which involved the synchronization of phonographs and projectors. These systems were hounded by problems: the phonograph's limited capacity for amplification, the restricted length and poor sound quality of recordings, problems in synchronization between phonographs and projectors, and substantial start-up costs. By the 1920s competing technologies in the United States and Germany had solved these problems either by perfecting the sound-on-disc approach (Vitaphone in the United States) or by creating optical sound-on-film systems (Tri-Ergon in Germany and Phonofilm in the United States). Inventors in the Soviet Union and Japan would not be far behind.

The conversion to sound and the role of popular song

Music played a key role in what happened next. In an attempt to get an edge on the competition, Warner Bros. invested in the Vitaphone process to upgrade the musical accompaniment for its films. The New York Philharmonic was hired to record the score for the studio's first Vitaphone feature, *Don Juan* (1926), which screened with loudspeakers positioned in the orchestra pit. Al Jolson's ad-libbed patter in Warner Bros.' next Vitaphone feature, a musical titled *The Jazz Singer* (1927), ushered in the sound revolution. Although it was dialogue that drove the new technology, it was the genre of the musical that that most fully exploited it. In the United States, important refinements in sound production were developed in musicals—postsynchronization in *Hallelujah* (1929) and double-channel recording in *Applause* (1929). The performance of song and dance was quickly embraced in Europe as a showcase for the new sound technology, along with a new set of performers: Marlene Dietrich in *The Blue Angel* (1930) in Germany; Josephine Baker in *Princess Tam Tam* (1935) in France; Jessie Matthews in *Evergreen* (1934) in England.

Around the globe, musicals provided a platform for the development of national film industries and the expression of national culture. Popular song would prove a key factor. In Hispanic and Lusophone cinemas, musicals were customized with indigenous popular musics: the tangueras of Argentina in *Adiós Buenos Aires* (1938); the chanchadas of Brazil with roots in Carnaval and Afro-Brazilian samba in *Alô Alô Carnaval* (1936); the canción ranchera of Mexico with the distinctive mariachi ensemble in *Allá en el Rancho Grande* (1936); Cuban zarzuela, a fusion of Spanish zarzuela, Italian opera, French operetta, US Tin Pan Alley, and Afro-Cubano music, in the Cuban–Mexican co-production *María la O* (1948); the copla andaluza of Spain, songs based on Andalusian melodies and rhythms, in *Morena Clara* (1936); and Portuguese fado, highly emotive songs with melancholic themes, in *A Severa* (1931), Portugal's first talkie. Musicals proved so profitable that even in nonmusical genres it was common to include popular music. Songs were interpolated into dramas in Mexico such as *María Candelaria* (1944) and *Flor Silvestre* (1943), in Spain *Nuestra Culpable* (1937), in Cuba *Embrujo antillano* (1947) and *Aventurera* (1950), and in Portugal

Fado, Historías duma Cantadeira (1947). Popular song and the related media of the radio and recording industries mediated national identity across Latin America, Spain, and Portugal in the 1930s and 1940s and helped to forge modern national culture.

Even in the Stalinist-era Soviet Union, the musical was an important and popular genre, although any connection to the Hollywood musical with its decadent connotations was downplayed. Depending on established stars of the recording industry and infused with Soviet ideology, musicals set on rural collectives such as *The Tractor Drivers* (1939), or in urban settings such as *The Happy Guys* (1934), incorporated the performance of original songs, Soviet military and patriotic songs, and folk music. Popular music and folk songs were also inserted into nonmusical genres. "How Good Life Will Be" and "If Only I Had Mountains of Gold" were interpolated into politically charged dramas such as *Alone* (1931) and *Golden Mountains* (1931). Even the historical epic *Alexander Nevsky* (1938) has some impressive songs performed by off-screen choruses and soloists. Song, both in and out of musicals, would prove a distinctive feature of Soviet films for decades to come.

Indigenous song, either borrowed from Chinese opera or the popular repertoire or originally composed in traditional or popular idioms, filled the soundtracks of Chinese-language films and produced some of the most popular songs of the twentieth century in China, Hong Kong, and Taiwan. But the films in which these songs appeared did not follow the Hollywood model. Indigenous songs were interpolated into a variety of genres and often featured actors who could sing. Chinese opera would prove a particularly durable musical source, and the first sound film in China, *The Songstress Red Peony* (1931), used four songs from Chinese opera, dubbed by the opera master Mei Lanfang, famous for his portrayals of female characters on the opera stage. In the 1930s, leftist filmmakers would insert revolutionary songs alongside those from opera in films such as *Big Road* (1935) and

Street Angel (1937). In *Street Angel*, the audience is invited to sing along to lyrics on the screen. In Hong Kong, early sound films such as *White Golden Dragon* (1933) mined Chinese opera for stories, stars, and, of course, music. The first Taiwanese sound film was also based in opera, *Six Talents' Romance of the West Chamber* (1955).

Song was central to the development of sound film. But, as in Chinese-language films, song in many parts of the world functioned in a radically different way from Hollywood. The film industry in India provides a dramatic case. The powerful traditions of song and dance in nineteenth-century Indian theater paved the way. Sound films became saturated with song, some with more than fifty musical numbers! These early sound films were produced by various regional film industries and in various dialects—*Alam Ara* (1931) in Hindi; *Kalidasa* (1931) in Tamil; and *Bhakta Prahlad* (1931) in Telegu—and songs within the films were performed in a variety of languages: Tamil, Telegu, Hindi, Bengali, and Sanskrit. The performance of indigenous song became a defining part of the film landscape throughout India but especially in Bollywood, the Hindi cinema industry centered in Bombay (now Mumbai), where it became a virtual requirement to include multiple performances of song (and dance) in every film, regardless of genre.

In the process, a hybrid and synthetic musical form was forged in Bollywood, the film song, influenced by classical Indian Karnatic and Hindustani rāgas, popular folk musics, and Western harmonic influences, and a new way of performing it, with playback singers, popular artists who prerecorded the songs to be lip-synched by the actors. Many of the playback singers, particularly Lata Mangeshkar and her sister Asha Bhosle, developed enormous fan bases, becoming more popular than the actors. Mangeshkar's career spanned seven decades, Bhosle's is going on eight, and between them they have recorded more than 120,000 songs.

Composers of film songs, known as music directors, were featured prominently in a film's advertising and were often paid more than the director. Important music directors in early sound film include C. Ramchandra, who drew on traditional music from the Uttar Pradesh region and mixed it with Western swing, jazz, and Latin American rhythms in films like *Abela* (1951); the team of Shankar–Jaikishan, who scored the sensationally popular *Awaara* (1951) and worked from the 1950s until the 1980s; and Saraswati Devi, the first woman music director who joined Bombay Talkies Film Company in 1935, who scored *Achut Kanya* (1936) and when it proved a hit sustained a successful career in music inside and outside the studio until the 1950s.

The first film songs were performed by small ensembles composed of many of the same instruments that were used in the silent era, including the harmonium and tabla. By the 1930s, the violin, cello, mandolin, piano, organ, and clarinet were added, as well as Indian instruments including the veena, *pakhawaj, jal tarang, bansuri*, and sitar. By the 1950s, studio orchestras expanded to more than one hundred players. Film songs were so important in Bollywood that they came first in the production process: the job of the screenwriter was to provide a narrative framework on which to hang these songs. This process of fitting the narrative to the songs became known as picturization.

Bollywood gave rise to a new model for including song, different from the way song became institutionalized in Hollywood and leading to some fundamental differences in the reception of film itself. Bollywood cinema, and many other national cinemas like it, inverts the relationship between narrative exposition and performance central to the integrated Hollywood musical where narrative is prioritized and songs are integrated into the storyline. In Bollywood cinema, the songs are prioritized and the narrative operates in relation to them with storylines picturizing the songs. Further, in the Hollywood musical, the technologies of song performance (prerecording, dubbing, postproduction processes) are carefully hidden so as not to disturb the illusion of reality. In Hindi cinema, the technology is exposed. Songs are not sung by the onscreen characters but dubbed by playback singers, a fact well known by audiences, producing a distinctly different form of cinematic pleasure from that on offer from Hollywood, one not contingent on a suspension of disbelief and hinging instead on cinema's artifice.

For a significant portion of the world, Bollywood has proved more influential than Hollywood. Many national cinemas in Asia and Africa share with Hindi cinema similar assumptions about indigenous music and the relationship of narrative to performance. The earliest film musicals in Turkey were fashioned after Hollywood models featuring ballads and, interestingly, tangos! But these were soon replaced with a hybrid form created by rescoring and adding song performances to existing films imported from Bollywood and Egypt.

The first Iranian sound film was actually produced in Bombay. *The Lor Girl* (1933) included Persian singing and dancing to original songs composed expressly for the film. These songs, however, did not express characters' emotions or further the narrative but provided opportunities to showcase songs composed with classical Persian poetry that addressed existential issues and philosophical ideas familiar to Iranian audiences. *Film Farsi* developed after World War II in Iran, incorporating song and dance into various genres, creating genre-benders like musical melodramas. *Sharmsar* (1950), one such example, featured a dramatic performance and songs by Delkash, a popular Iranian songstress.

Soon, the performances of songs were dubbed by popular singers, as they were in Hindi cinema, and actors established relationships with singers who would provide their on-screen voices. In fact, in the postwar era, the inclusion of Persian singing and dancing became so obligatory that foreign films were altered to meet the expectations of Persian audiences. Thus when the Hollywood blockbuster *Ben-Hur* (1959) was screened, songs performed by Iranian singers were interpolated into the film.

Egypt quickly developed into one of the largest film industries in the Arab world, and as in the Hindi industry, the performance of song was a crucial element. Films of various genres with interpolated musical performances constituted a significant portion of the industry's output and commercial successes well into the 1960s.

Song and dance were important facets of Egyptian culture long before sound film arrived, and Egyptian sound cinema tapped a number of popular performers for its growing industry. The musical melting pot that produced the Egyptian film song—Latin American rhythms, themselves influenced by African music, Western instrumentation and song structure, and traditional Arab song—can be heard in films such as *The White Rose* (1934) and *Wedad* (1936), which made film stars of the popular singers and recording artists Mohamed Abdel-Wahab and Umm Kulthum. In *Victory of Youth* (1941) and *Honeymoon* (1946), Lebanese and Syrian musical elements were added to the mix.

Among the most popular postwar Egyptian films were love stories told against a background of musical performances in such films as *The Flirtation of Girls* (1949), with the popular singer Layla Morad. When several Arab film industries began incorporating musical performances later in the twentieth century, they modeled their films on this Egyptian model: in Lebanon, *The Seller of the Rings* (1965), *Safar Barlek* (1966), and *The Daughter of the Guardian* (1968); in Morocco, *Life Is a Struggle* (1968) and *Silence Is a One-Way Street* (1973); and in Tunisia, *Screams* (1972).

The development of the background score

The performance of song generated a number of different practices in early sound film. Background music followed a similar trajectory. Background music—what is traditionally called the score—refers to the music playing in the background, that is, not foregrounded in the film through performance or visually produced within the film. Different film practices treated background music in different ways: from Bollywood, where background music was so overshadowed by film songs that the composers who created it were often uncredited, to Turkish cinema, where musical scores were comprised of selections from vinyl recordings, a process known as upholstering; from Chinese-language film and *film Farsi*, where *bricolage* construction mixed a variety of musical sources, to the Soviet cinema where principles of montage were applied to the score. And then there was Hollywood, which generated a highly codified institutional practice for the composition and placement of background music.

The question of what to do about background music at the onset of sound cinema was characterized by an eclectic set of responses. There were some attempts to preserve silent traditions. Charlie Chaplin's early sound films, *City Lights* (1931) and *Modern Times* (1936), had virtually no dialogue or sound effects and were scored with continuous music. In Japan, the persistence of silent production continued well into the 1930s, promoted by benshi trying vainly to stave off synchronized sound and unemployment. Ironically, now that technology made possible the economical reproduction of first-class musical accompaniment, many films used no background music at all or went to absurd lengths to justify its presence. In Josef von Sternberg's otherwise gritty Hollywood crime drama, *Thunderbolt* (1929), prisoners just happen to be practicing music in their cells (von Suppe's *Poet and Peasant*, no less) during the film's climactic escape sequence.

There were innovative responses, too. In Hollywood, Hugo Riesenfeld combined two musical mediums, a jazz band and a small orchestra, for distinctive effects in *Sunrise* (1927). In France, Maurice Jaubert used electronic manipulation to produce an arresting cue for a slow-motion sequence in Jean Vigo's *Zéro de conduite* (1933). In the Netherlands, Hanns Eisler scored Joris

Ivens's documentary *New Earth* (1934) using naturalistic sound for the machines but music for the humans. In Britain, Arthur Benjamin experimented with orchestration to compensate for problems in early sound recording, reducing the number of strings and even creating pizzicato effects from tuba and piano. And in Berlin, at the German Film Research Institute, filmic equivalents of musical phenomena were identified to facilitate synchronization between the two (such as the dolly-in and dolly-out for crescendo and decrescendo and superimpositions for dissonance). Perhaps it was these experiments that Arnold Schoenberg was thinking of when he was approached by Irving Thalberg at MGM to score *The Good Earth* (1936). The story goes that he was interested if he could complete the score first and have the film shot to fit his music, retain total control of the soundtrack, and earn $50,000, twice the going rate for Hollywood's top composers. The answer was no. Schoenberg did complete some sketches for the film, but in the end, he did not write the score or any other in Hollywood.

Very early in the sound period, composers in the Soviet Union treated the score as an element of montage. Influenced no doubt by the 1928 "Statement on Sound," Soviet filmmakers explored the emotional, intellectual, and ideological effects of music that created disjunction with the image. Believing that revolutionary art demands revolutionary practice, Soviet filmmakers extended a revolutionary aesthetic to the score. In Pudovkin's *Deserter*, for instance, the despair and suicide of a starving worker caught stealing bread is alarmingly at odds with the jazzy melody and Latin-inflected rhythms of Yuri Shaporin's score. Earlier in the film, as contraband news is disseminated via newspapers, a jaunty waltz starts and stops, as if a phonograph needle was skipping over scratches on a phonograph recording. At the Communist Party parade, shots of workers and soldiers are accompanied by Bizet's *Carmen*. In Grigori Kozintsev and Leonid Trauberg's *Alone*, Dmitri Shostakovich scores a scene in which the heroine sobs out her agony to a party official accompanied by light-hearted, percussive music featuring a calliope-like street organ. In Sergei Yutkevich's *Golden Mountains*, Shostakovich scores a sequence of men trampling through thick mud with the crisp sound of a xylophone and percussion and accompanies unsympathetic bourgeoisie with Hawaiian guitars. Such musical and narrative disjunctions were designed to undercut conventional bourgeois emotional attachments on the part of the audience, opening up viewers to the revolutionary aesthetic of these early Soviet sound films.

In Japan, Akira Kurosawa was much influenced by Soviet filmmakers. Kurosawa took a firm hand in the creation of the scores for his films, and several of his postwar features are marked by examples of disjunctive music: the cheery "Cuckoo Waltz," an American folk tune used distinctively in John Ford westerns, assailing the gangster who has just learned he is doomed in the contemporary crime drama *Drunken Angel* (1948); a life-and-death telephone call accompanied by a tango or a tense confrontation between cop and criminal accompanied by a sonatina on a piano in the contemporary policier *Stray Dog* (1949); a jazzy saxophone riff accompanying bumbling medieval peasants in the period action film *The Hidden Fortress* (1958); the shock effect of traditional Shinto music paired with Wagner's "Wedding March" during a Japanese bridal ceremony, or mamboesque pop music combined with a Buddhist monk's chanting at a funeral in *The Bad Sleep Well* (1960); or the use of bongos and big band swing in the period action film *Yojimbo* (1961).

Another aesthetic was also shaping up in Japan. Although the first sound films depended on popular songs to fill the soundtrack, composers from the concert hall such as Yamada Kosaku and Kami Kyosuke were soon drawn to film scoring. A lively debate ensued over the place of Western music. An important figure here is Fumio Hayasaka, who believed that films should use Japanese music. His score for Kenji Mizoguchi's *Ugetsu* (1954) uses *geza* music of Kabuki theater and his score for Mizoguchi's *The Crucified Lovers* (1954) features prominent use of Japanese percussion, fusing the boundary between music and sound. Hayasaka, memorably, scored a series of films for Kurosawa and sometimes found himself in conflict with the director over Kurosawa's fondness for Western music. For *Rashomon* (1950), Kurosawa insisted on a bolero and gave Hayasaka Ravel's *Bolero* to emulate—which he did. But Hayasaka was also able to incorporate *gagaku*, traditional music of the Japanese Imperial Court, performed on such traditional instruments as the *sho* (mouth organ) and the *wagon* (a type of zither). Popular song did not disappear from Japanese film, however. Tapping into the enormous popularity of the hit tune, "The Fragrance of the Night," Kon Ichikawa's 1951 film of the same name recycles the song instrumentally throughout the score, including as a leitmotif for the lovers. Yoshiko Yamaguchi, the singer-turned-actress who recorded the song, appears as the female protagonist and even hums the song at one point.

Bricolage scores embodied yet another practice for background music, one in which various kinds of music, both borrowed and originally composed, indigenous and foreign, converged in a kind of pastiche. These bricolage scores often fulfilled the functions common to silent film accompaniment, particularly the creation of mood and atmosphere. In Iran, film composers created bricolage scores from traditional Persian music, original composition, Western concert music, and surprisingly cues from Hollywood film scores. In Iran, after World War II, "Tara's Theme" from *Gone with the Wind* (1939) became so popular that it turned up in numerous Iranian soundtracks. In the golden age of Turkish cinema (1948–60), so-called upholstery music operated on bricolage principles. Scores were created from recordings typically chosen by sound engineers and exploited indigenous popular music, Western concert music, jazz, and pop.

Other Arab and African filmmaking traditions similarly exploited bricolage scores combining Hollywood-style film music; indigenous music, both traditional and popular; and original composition. In the films of the Egyptian director Youssef Chahine, Hollywood-style background music was often used in calculated counterpoint to traditional Arab music. In *Always in My Heart* (1945), Egyptian director Salah Abu-Seif wove a folk song throughout the film as a leitmotif, and it became his signature tune in subsequent work.

In Shanghai, film music also gravitated toward bricolage. Composers Er Nie in *New Woman* (1935) and Luting He in *City Scenes* (1935) and *Street Angel* (1937) mixed Chinese folk and popular music with Western musical styles. It was not uncommon to hear Strauss waltzes, Western sacred music, US big band music, Latin American dance music, and indigenous Chinese traditional and popular music along with originally composed music in the score. Although initially dismissed by critics as ineffectual, these early sound film scores have been re-evaluated by scholars such as Sue Tuohy and Emilie (Yueh-yu) Yeh. They argue that these scores performed a critical role in envisioning China's future by juxtaposing, musically, China's past and its colonial present, creating a musical dialogue between East and West, often fraught with ambiguity, about social change.

In Socialist-era Mongolia, film scores were symphonic, not surprising as they were heavily influenced by filmmaking in the Soviet Union where symphonic scores were standard practice. But Mongolian film scores relied on bricolage as a structuring principle and thus were able to incorporate a variety of different types of music and influences: traditional Mongolian music (often through utilizing the pentatonic scale), military marches, Russian accordion music, revolutionary Socialist songs, Buddhist temple music, popular music derived from Anglo-American models, and by the 1970s even jazz.

In Bollywood, where film songs became a unique and enduring form of popular music and were marketed in advance of a film's release, the background score itself was pushed, well, into the background. It was typically a bricolage of traditional Indian musical elements and Western-style melodies and instrumentation.

The classical Hollywood film score

In the United States, a model for the use of background music evolved in classical Hollywood cinema, a term that refers to an institutional practice for the production of narrative film realized through a powerful studio system, which flourished from the 1930s through the early 1960s in and around Hollywood. As part of this practice, a set of conventions for the use of background music evolved in the 1930s, harnessing some of the most powerful effects of music both to support the seamless storytelling that Hollywood perfected and to engage the audience uncritically in the world that the story creates.

The classical Hollywood film score revolved around a core set of functions: music to sustain unity by covering potential gaps in the narrative chain occasioned by editing (such as transitions between sequences and especially montages); music to emphasize narrative action through coordination of music and image, often through mickey mousing, matching screen action explicitly to the rhythms and shape of the music (so named because it was developed for Disney animation); music to control connotation by fleshing out mood and atmosphere, establishing time and geographic place, and delineating characters' subjectivity; music to accompany dialogue, called underscoring, through the subordination of music to speech; and music to connect the audience to the filmic world through an appeal to emotion. Music was rendered unobtrusive by masking its entrances and exits, but it was none the less powerful because it was relegated to the perceptual background.

The classical Hollywood film score coalesced through the work of three composers in the 1930s, Max Steiner, Erich Wolfgang Korngold, and Alfred Newman, whose scores for *King Kong* (1933), *The Adventures of Robin Hood* (1938), and *Wuthering Heights* (1939), respectively, are among the most accomplished in the form. They were joined by others, notably Dimitri Tiomkin, Miklós Rózsa, Bronislau Kaper, and Franz Waxman. All but Newman had immigrated from Europe, many fleeing Hitler and the rise of fascism.

A key element in the classical Hollywood film score was its Romantic idiom. In the 1930s when scoring conventions developed in Hollywood, modernism was in full swing in concert halls and popular music was surging in popularity because of the growth of the radio and recording industries. And yet Romanticism was embraced as the vehicle for Hollywood to meet its musical needs. It is interesting to consider why. Romanticism (as opposed to baroque or modern music) privileges melody, an accessible musical structure for listeners, and the privileging of melody meshed nicely with the privileging of narrative in classical Hollywood cinema. Romanticism also had at its disposal the leitmotif, an extremely adaptable mechanism for accessing listeners, unifying the score, and responding to a film's dramatic needs. Additionally, many of the influential scores of the silent era were already relying on Romantic models.

The expanded size of the Romantic orchestra matched both Hollywood's grandiose conception of itself and the musical tastes of its producers. Many of the composers in Hollywood had been born in Europe and were trained in Romanticism. (But then, had Hollywood not been interested in Romanticism, it would not have attracted these composers.) Caryl Flinn theorizes that it was Hollywood's assembly-line mode of production and its accompanying artistic frustration that fostered Hollywood composers' attraction to Romanticism, with its focus on the individual and its belief in the transformative nature of creativity and art's transcendence over social and historical reality, not the lived reality of composers employed in studio music departments.

Erich Wolfgang Korngold and *The Adventures of Robin Hood*

Korngold's score for *The Adventures of Robin Hood* is a consummate example of classical scoring principles. Korngold evokes, without actually adopting, late medieval music (notably in the banquet sequence in Nottingham Castle), recasting medieval English balladry into a Romantic tapestry. But it is in his use of leitmotifs that Korngold is at his most brilliant.

King Richard's leitmotif, which comes to embody England itself, is first heard in the stable harmony of E♭ major. Richard is absent from the film, off on the Crusades. His leitmotif is heard in a series of variations in various keys from major to minor, returning to E♭ major only upon Richard's dramatic reappearance in England at the end of the film. The leitmotif for the villainous Guy of Gisbourne is built on the disquieting intervals of ascending major sevenths and minor ninths. The leitmotif for the Merry Men of Sherwood Forest is well established by the time they appear at the archery contest in disguise. Korngold cleverly "disguises" their leitmotif as well, omitting the middle notes of the melody until the Merry Men reveal themselves. The innocence of Maid Marian is characterized in a leitmotif of simple harmonies and a delicate melody with a high degree of repetition. The Norman oppression leitmotif is built on dissonance (descending minor seconds).

Leitmotifs also connect the characters to each other in interesting ways. The leitmotif for Robin and Marian, which functions as their love theme, grows out of King Richard's leitmotif (they share an opening ascending fifth), connecting Robin and Marian's love of king and country to their love for each other. It is King Richard's leitmotif that we hear during a key sequence in which Robin and Marian begin to fall in love and King Richard's leitmotif that plays a major role in the balcony scene where the couple declares their love. Even more interesting are the links between Robin and Guy, notably the ascending sevenths and ninths that can be heard introducing Robin's leitmotif when he confronts Guy at Nottingham Castle, suggesting intriguing similarities between hero and villain. In *The Adventures of Robin Hood*, key elements of Western tonality are exploited in the leitmotivic plan for the score, contributing mightily to the development of character and theme.

The Romantic idiom and its symphonic deployment were utilized by many a composer working outside Hollywood (and by some who were later lured to Hollywood) well into the mid-twentieth century. A short list would include William Walton for *Henry V* (1944) in Britain; Nino Rota for *The Leopard* (1963) in Italy; and Luvsanjambyn Mördorj and Bilegiin Damdinsüren for *Tsogt Taig* (1945) in Mongolia.

New idioms, new instruments

With the influx of new composers to Hollywood in the 1940s and 1950s, more contemporary musical idioms joined Romanticism: jazz, serialism, and modernism. In Hollywood, jazz infiltrated the film score in the 1950s and gravitated toward film noir, crime film, and urban melodramas in scores such as Alex North's for *A Streetcar Named Desire* (1951), Elmer Bernstein's for *The Man with the Golden Arm* (1956) and *Sweet Smell of Success* (1957) featuring the Chico Hamilton Quintet, John Lewis's for *Odds against Tomorrow* (1959) featuring the Modern Jazz Quartet, Henry Mancini's for *Touch of Evil* (1958), and Quincy Jones's for *The Pawnbroker* (1964). A number of prominent jazz artists in the United States have been tapped to score films: Duke Ellington for *Anatomy of a Murder* (1959) and *Paris Blues* (1960), Charles Mingus for *Shadows* (1958), and Herbie Hancock for *Death Wish*

4. Muir Mathieson conducts William Walton's score for *Hamlet* (1948). When film scores were recorded, the conductor watched the film projected on a giant screen behind the orchestra.

(1974). Miles Davis, the legendary jazz trumpeter, scored the French film *Elevator to the Gallows* (1958), in which he improvised the entire score supposedly in a single night. In Poland, Krzysztof Komeda scored *Knife in the Water* (1962), and in Japan, Toshiro Mayuzumi scored *When a Woman Ascends the Stairs* (1960) with jazz. Although scores composed entirely of jazz are not common, jazzy melodies, instruments, and rhythms turn up in the musical vocabularies of many film composers.

Jazz was initially associated with urban decadence, and the extent to which these associations cling to jazz is an open question among film scholars. Krin Gabbard, for instance, points out that many Hollywood jazz scores continue to reflect racism and sexism. Jazz scores turned up sporadically in films post-1970. Jazz is the subject of Clint Eastwood's Charlie Parker biopic *Bird* (1988) and

Spike Lee's fictional drama, *Mo' Better Blues* (1990), and both scores are heavily influenced by jazz, scored by Lennie Niehaus and Bill Lee, respectively. Jazz saxophonist Joshua Redman scored *Vanya on 42nd Street* (1994), and jazz drummer Antonio Sánchez scored *Birdman* (2014).

Serialism, also called twelve-tone music, would make its mark in mid-century. Serialism is a method of composition associated with Arnold Schoenberg in which all twelve pitches in the Western scale are used equally to avoid establishing any tonality. Listen for it in Leonard Rosenman's score for *The Cobweb* (1955) as well as in Scott Bradley's scores for Tom and Jerry cartoons at MGM. Quipped Bradley, "I hope that Dr. Schoenberg will forgive me for using *his system* to produce funny music, but even the boys in the orchestra laughed when we were recording it."

The unconventional rhythms, the intimate and unusual configurations of instruments, and the unexpected and often dissonant harmonies of modernism had a larger impact. Modernism was writ large in Leonard Rosenman's scores for *East of Eden* (1955) and *Rebel without a Cause* (1955), Leonard Bernstein's for *On the Waterfront* (1954), Alex North's for *Spartacus* (1960), and, of all places, the score for Walt Disney's animated feature *Bambi* (1942), where Edward Plumb channels Stravinsky's *The Firebird* in the fire sequence that destroys the forest. But modernism could also be heard in numerous film scores that exploited modernist effects for specific purposes, like Franz Waxman's use of the theremin to suggest altered states in his scores for *Spellbound* (1945) and *The Lost Weekend* (1945).

Most potently, modernism was exploited in a series of scores Bernard Herrmann composed for Alfred Hitchcock. These scores bear the imprint of modernism: striking instrumentation such as the all-string ensemble for *Psycho* (1960) or the all-brass ensemble for the discarded *Torn Curtain* (1966) score; arresting rhythms such as the habanera from *Vertigo* (1958) or the fandango from *North by Northwest* (1950); dissonant harmonies (the shrieking violin glissandi in the shower scene from *Psycho*) and polytonality (the famous *Vertigo* chord), two perfectly conventional tonal chords played simultaneously.

Outside Hollywood

In the golden age of Mexican cinema, modernism mixed with traditional Mexican corrido-canciones in the scores of Silvestre Revueltas. A modernist composer, Revueltas brought techniques such as dissonance and polyrhythms to the orchestral portions of the soundtrack of *Vámanos con Pancho Villa!* (1936), which alternated with and sometimes mixed with traditional songs such as "La Adelita." In *La noche de los Mayas* (1939), Revueltas again produced a score that blended a traditional Mayan melody with modernism, particularly in the arresting polyrhythms of the fandango, moments of dissonance, and a battery of Latin percussion including bongos, congas, tom-toms, gourds, conch shells, and log drums. Arranged into a concert suite after Revuelta's death, *La noche de los Mayas* (1959) enjoys a second life on the concert stage, where it was performed as recently as May 2022 by the Los Angeles Philharmonic conducted by Gustavo Dudamel.

Modernism became something of a mark of authenticity, a sign of the suspicion of and refusal to adopt normative filmic conventions, in the cinema of auteur directors in the 1960s and in the international film community where they circulated. Auteur directors often labeled as modernist, such as Michelangelo Antonioni, Ingmar Bergman, Luis Buñuel, Alain Resnais, Claude Chabrol, and Carlos Saura, fashioned films that used music sparingly. Avoiding many of film music's traditional functions such as establishing mood and channeling emotion, composers for the films of these modernist directors produced something akin to

Brecht's noted distanciation effect with music devoid of emotional triggers for the audience. Hanns Eisler, in the score for Resnais's documentary *Night and Fog* (1955), undercut powerful images of Nazis on parade with unexpected pizzicato strings. Luis de Pablo, in the score for Saura's *The Garden of Delights* (1970), signaled a character's mental breakdown through *musique concréte*, an avant-garde practice using nonmusical sounds to make music. Alain Robbe-Grillet, who wrote the screenplay for *Last Year at Marienbad* (1961), had wanted only noises captured on location for the accompaniment. That, however, is not what he got. Instead, the composer Francis Seyrig provided a fugue for organ and Romantically inflected orchestral music, creating a lush but disorienting effect given the sterility of the stiff, formally dressed characters and endless hallways.

The French New Wave is an excellent example of the ways in which unconventional choices found expression in the film score in the second half of the twentieth century. Directors such as François Truffaut, Chabrol, Jacques Rivette, Resnais, and especially Jean-Luc Godard sought iconoclastic scores for their fresh and often revolutionary approaches to film content, construction, and style. Chabrol and Truffaut established long-term collaborations with composers to give their films a distinctive sound (Pierre Jansen scored more than thirty films for Chabrol; Georges Delerue scored eleven for Truffaut), but perhaps the most striking examples of New Wave scores are those for several of Godard's films: Martial Solal's jazzy score for *Breathless* (1959); Michel Legrand's theme and variations for *Vivre sa vie* (1962), which Godard abruptly and arbitrarily stopped mid-phrase at the end of the film; *Weekend* (1967), which features a concert pianist in a barnyard; and *Sauve qui peut (la vie)* (1980), where characters in a shoot-out run past the musicians playing Gabriel Yared's score.

Using stylishly modernist effects, serialism, and *musique concréte*, combined with elements of popular music, Mexican and Sicilian folk influences, Celtic song, and Gregorian chant, Ennio Morricone created a series of memorable scores for Sergio Leone's spaghetti westerns of the 1960s. In *The Good, The Bad, and the Ugly* (1966), Morricone uses conventional melody played on an electric guitar, an ocarina (an ancient flute), and a harmonica, along with much more unconventional types of scoring including whistling, yodeling, grunting, vocalizations at times unrecognizable as human, whipcracks, and gunshots. Morricone turned his back on the Hollywood conventions for western film scores that emphasized the melodic contours and harmonic textures of folk song and hymnody. In the process, Morricone provided a new model for the western film score. Marco Beltrami's score for the Hollywood western *3:10 to Yuma* (2007) is an example of Morricone's continuing legacy to the genre.

The German New Wave also uses music unconventionally, gravitating toward pastiche in its scores, which quote everything from Bach to the Beatles. Music calls attention to itself, performed in exaggerated, skewed, or clichéd ways or yanked out of context into startling relationships with the images. Caryl Flinn argues that these disquieting relationships call authenticity itself into question and force viewers into critical awareness of the issues of history, memory, and identity tied up with Germany's past.

Peer Raben, who composed a series of scores for Rainer Werner Fassbinder (and helped choose the preexisting songs), echoes earlier modernists in using music to shock. In *The Marriage of Maria Braun* (1979), Raben arranges a Nazi soldier's song for xylophone and glockenspiel, deliberately invoking childhood and innocence. In *Chinese Roulette* (1976), Raben uses dance forms to accompany a character who cannot walk without crutches.

For a series of films by Werner Herzog, the music group Popol Vuh (named after a Mayan book of mythology) created a series of arresting cues, many generated electronically and some using native instruments, which obscured precise ethnic origin: the quasi-religious Buddhist chanting (by the Bavarian State Opera chorus) in *Aguirre: The Wrath of God* (1972), set in the Amazon rainforest during the Spanish conquest of the New World, or the quasi-Gregorian chanting, accompanied by a sitar, in *Nosferatu* (1979), Herzog's remake of F. W. Murnau's 1922 vampire film.

The German New Wave's iconoclastic approach to the score has been taken up (and amplified) by the Austrian director Michael Haneke. In his films such as *The Piano Teacher* (2001) and *Funny Games* (1997, and its English-language remake, 2007), music is used in unconventional ways. It is generally sparing and/or fragmented, or disturbingly loud or soft with radical shifts in volume, or distracting and disruptive, all of which function to thwart emotional connection with viewers.

In Japan in the 1960s, Tôru Takemitsu created innovative scores for a number of films. Takemitsu, the leading composer of concert music in Japan, had developed a style fusing musical elements of East and West, which proved accessible to the international art-house audience. Nevertheless, many of his scores are highly experimental and bring an unexpected edge to what listeners expect to hear (or not hear). In *Kwaidan* (1964) Takemitsu used *musique concréte* to great effect in the representation of ghostly presences; in *Woman of the Dunes* (1964) he electronically manipulated the recording process to create a dreamlike wash of sound. Takemitsu's film work is also marked by a distinctive placement of both sound and silence, and he is sometimes credited with the sound design as well as the score. In Kurosawa's *Ran* (1985), sound disappears in the graphically violent battle sequence, replaced by an extended symphonic cue. The disturbing contrast between the beautiful, elegiac melody and the scene of slaughter is abruptly halted when a gunshot is heard. The music disappears at this point, and the soundtrack is filled with the grotesque sounds of death. Explains Takemitsu, "I want to give sounds the freedom to breathe."

In the 1950s, Indian directors, working outside the Hindi industry, reached out to the new international audience. One of them, Satyajit Ray, working in the Bengali industry centered in Calcutta (now Kolkata), quickly established himself as one of the new auteurs. Unlike Bollywood, Bengali cinema used Western musics, including US pop music, Latin American music, Iberian music, Western concert music, and Hollywood scoring techniques. Further, music was used more conventionally in Bengali cinema than in Bollywood, with musical performances more narratively justified and relegated to naturalistic settings as nightclubs, parties, or dream sequences. Ray claimed, "If I were asked to find room for six songs in a story that is not expressly a 'musical,' I would have to throw up my hands and give up."

Ray's Apu trilogy, among his earliest films, was scored by Ravi Shankar. Shankar had traveled extensively in the West but used exclusively Indian instruments and concert and folk music traditions for his film scores, apparently to Ray's dismay. Ray would soon begin composing himself. Nevertheless, some of the most profoundly moving moments in Ray's oeuvre occur in Shankar's scores: in *Pather Panchali* (1955), when a returning father is told by his wife that their daughter has died, and the sound of their dialogue is replaced by the wail of the high-pitched *tar shehnai*, or in *Aparajito* (1956), when Apu's mother slaps Apu in the face, and their mutual shock is registered after the fact by percussion.

Chapter 6
A history of film music III: 1970-2022

By the 1970s, film industries around the world found themselves in rapidly changing terrain. The studio system had broken down and Hollywood was in the process of transformation. Audiences were diminishing and demographics were skewing younger. The rise of auteurism empowered directors. The art film promoted experimentation in film form and style. Film viewing became more global, with films from national industries outside Hollywood gaining more access to the marketplace. Filmmaking itself became more global, with funding, production, and distribution increasingly shared across national borders. The film score would respond to these changes.

Romanticism, joined mid-century by jazz, modernism, and serialism, made way for even newer idioms. Electronic and synthesized music became common. Popular music moved to the forefront of score production, especially rock 'n' roll, which began to be incorporated into or even constitute entire film scores. The compilation score proved a formidable challenge to the originally composed film score and eventually the compilation score became the dominant model. World music became increasingly audible. And film composing itself became a more global enterprise with composers, often with global backgrounds of their own, routinely hopping between different national film industries. In Hollywood and Bollywood, the large music departments capable of handling all aspects of a score's production were largely a thing of the past, and new institutions and institutional practices developed to fill the void. Composers became free agents, with some stepping up to create their own music studios, an interesting twist on outsourcing. And, as had been the case earlier, especially in the 1930s, composers suffered the fallout from political events beyond their control.

Old patterns, new practices

By the 1970s, the Romanticism that had proved so durable in the film scores of the Hollywood studio system had lost its luster. Although there were the occasional Romantic film scores, like Nino Rota's for the *Godfather I* and *II*, the scores that were garnering the most attention, from critics and audiences alike, explored other idioms such as minimalism and mediums such as electronic and synthesized music. The dramatic comeback of the Romantic idiom in a symphonic medium, sometimes referred to as neo-Romanticism, would be precipitated by John Williams with the phenomenal success of his scores for the *Star Wars* trilogy (1977–83), recorded for the film's soundtrack by the London Symphony. Neo-Romanticism in symphonic form remains in play to this day for big-budget, action-adventure blockbusters in Hollywood, such as *Dances with Wolves* (1990), the *Jurassic Park* franchise (1993–2022), and the *Harry Potter* franchise (2001–2011) and its spin-offs, many scored by John Williams.

Around the world, big-budget films on epic subjects have gravitated toward neo-Romantic scores: Patrick Doyle's for *Henry V* (1991) in Great Britain; Gabriel Yared's for *Camille Claudel* (1988) in France; and Ennio Morricone's for *Cinema Paradiso* (1988) in Italy. Even outside the West, the symphony orchestra and Romantic traditions have held a certain fascination and have been used, often in combination with indigenous harmonics and instruments, by Tôru Takemitsu for *Ran* (1985) in Japan; by Natsagiin Jantsannorov for *Mandukhai the Wise Queen* (1988) in Mongolia; by Zhao Jiping for *Red Firecracker, Green*

Firecracker (1994) in China; and by Tan Dun for *Crouching Tiger, Hidden Dragon* (2000) in Taiwan. But Romanticism would now have to share the (scoring) stage with newer musical idioms.

Minimalism is a style of music originating in the avant-garde. It minimizes musical material—restricted melodies, repetitive harmonies, arpeggiated chords—which is then developed through subtle and minimal changes to volume, texture, and timbre. Characterized by repetitive musical figures, which disturb conventional notions of rhythm and time, minimalism attracted widespread attention through the mesmeric film scores of Philip Glass. Avoiding emotional triggers, Glass's minimalist scores gravitate to the structure of the film, deliberately leaving audiences to respond emotionally on their own.

In his score for *Koyaansquatsi* (1982), Glass's groundbreaking crossover from the avant-garde into film, audiences were treated to a thrilling departure from what they were accustomed to, even in art films. With no traditional dialogue, the film showcased its score, which featured winds and keyboard with low brasses, strings (but no violins), and a choir singing wordless vocalizations in what would become Glass's musical signature: rapid arpeggios, slowly moving bass lines, and syncopated rhythms.

Glass went on to score a number of films as he pursued his concert career, including *The Thin Blue Line* (1988), *Mishima* (1985), *A Brief History of Time* (1991), *The Hours* (2002), *The Fog of War* (2003), and even a Marvel franchise film, *Fantastic Four* (with Marco Beltrami, 2015). Michael Nyman's collaboration with Peter Greenaway also exploits the distinctive techniques of minimalism, particularly in *The Draughtsman's Contract* (1982), where repetitive musical structures find their analogue in the narrative construction of the film.

Other composers have adopted minimalist aesthetics, often with a combination of orchestral and synthesized music in response to a film's subject matter: James Horner for *A Beautiful Mind* (2001), a film about a brilliant schizophrenic mathematician; Stephen Warbeck for *Proof* (2005), about the relationship between a brilliant but mentally disturbed mathematician and his daughter; Clint Mansell for *Requiem for a Dream* (2000), about the psychological breakdown of the mind under drug addiction; Mica Levi for *Under the Skin* (2013), about an alien disguised as a human woman. Even John Williams gets into the act with his score for *A.I.: Artificial Intelligence* (2001), about a robotic boy who wants to become human. Some minimalist scores are embedded in a compilation pop score, which makes for an interesting mix, as in *The Social Network* (2010), about the socially maladjusted computer nerd who founds Facebook. For *Her* (2013), about a man who falls in love with his computer's operating system, the Canadian rock band Arcade Fire scored the film with rearrangements of their own songs in a minimalist style. It might even be argued that Hans Zimmer incorporated elements of minimalism—limited musical material, repetition of melodic units, strong rhythmic pulse—for *Inception* (2010), whose plot revolves around the human unconscious.

The first completely electronic score was produced by Louis and Bebe Barron (credited with "electronic tonalities") for *Forbidden Planet* (1956). Influenced by musique concréte, the Barrons fashioned the score entirely out of sounds produced electronically and then manipulated in postrecording. Because its sound could be so alien and otherworldly, electronic scoring soon became associated with science fiction.

Akira Ifukube used electronic scoring in *Godzilla* (1956). Eduard Artemiev created an electronic score for *Solaris* (1972). And in some reverse engineering, Mica Levi created "electronic music" for *Under the Skin* by digitally manipulating the sound of acoustic instruments.

5. Louis and Bebe Barron produced the first completely electronic film score in their electronic music lab.

The first electronic instrument is generally considered to be the theremin, played by the movement of the performer's hands through radio waves. As early as 1930, Dmitri Shostakovich used it in *Odna* (1930), where it accompanied a windstorm. Soon it was adopted in Hollywood, memorably in Miklós Rózsa's scores for *Spellbound* (1945) and *The Lost Weekend* (1945), where its eerie sound connoted psychic breakdown, and in Bernard Herrmann's score for the science fiction classic *The Day the Earth Stood Still* (1951), where two theremins accompanied the alien. The association between the theremin and the genre has continued into the twenty-first century. More recent examples include *Ghostbusters* (1984), *Mars Attacks!* (1996), and *First Man* (2019), a biopic about Neil Armstrong, the first man on the moon.

The electronic instrument with the most far-reaching influence for the film score, however, is the synthesizer. Electronic music moved into high visibility with Giorgio Moroder's synthesized score for *Midnight Express* (1978) and Vangelis's for *Chariots of*

Fire (1981) and *Blade Runner* (1982). The synthesizer is an electronic instrument that can reproduce the sound of acoustic instruments through sampling, a kind of digital picture of a sound, which can then be manipulated. The synthesizer has often replaced acoustic instruments, and with them the musicians who played them. It has also made the sounds of instruments from all parts of the world more accessible. Gabriel Yared's score for *The English Patient* (1996), for example, uses a traditional symphony orchestra along with the synthesized sound of the *quanoun*, a traditional Middle Eastern stringed instrument. For *Malevil* (1980), Yared created the score from the synthesized sounds of nature, his own voice, the quanoun, and the oud, another traditional Middle Eastern instrument, an ancestor of the lute. The synthesizer has also allowed artists, not trained as composers, to create film scores, such as the director John Carpenter, whose own synthesized music can be heard in many of his films, including *Assault on Precinct 13* (1976), *Halloween* (1978), and *Escape from New York* (1981).

The most innovative use of the synthesizer has been to create sounds that a traditional orchestra cannot make. Many composers have experimented with its capabilities. David Shire uses the distorted sound of a synthesized piano in *The Conversation* (1974) to suggest the protagonist's mental instability. Quincy Jones synthesizes sounds of electronic wiretapping and mixes them with a jazz combo in the score for *The Anderson Tapes* (1971). Cliff Martinez uses a synthesizer to create a kind of musical ambient sound throughout *Traffic* (2000) and to produce an otherworldly effect for the last scene of the film, of all things a baseball game. Hans Zimmer brought synthesized scores into the mainstream. His signature, much copied, is the combination of synthesized music (and recently electronic sound) with orchestral music in some of the most recognizable film scores of the twenty-first century: *Gladiator* (with Lisa Gerrard, 2000), *Pirates of the Caribbean: Dead Man's Chest* (2006), *The Dark Knight* trilogy (2005–12), *Sherlock Holmes* (2009), *Interstellar* (2014), *Dunkirk*

(2017), *Blade Runner 2049* (2017), and *Dune* (2021). In many film industries throughout the world, because they can be economical, synthesized scores have become the norm.

A parallel development has been the integration of sound design into the musical score where what had been traditionally defined as sound effects are now treated as musical elements to be integrated into the score. The score for *Dune* combines Zimmer's trademark synthesized and percussive music with novel sounds, some created with conventional instruments (cello, Irish whistles, Indian bamboo flutes, bagpipes), some by a female choir's wordless vocalizations (one singer recorded her voice in her closet in Brooklyn during the pandemic), entirely new instruments (a contrabass duduk) created for the score, and unconventional noises (scraping metal, springs, sawblades). For one cue, Zimmer wanted to capture the sound of sand.

Popular music and rock 'n' roll

The audience for film was changing, and by the 1970s those changes were becoming pronounced. Audiences were getting younger. And, more concerning, they were diminishing— a downward trend that began after World War II and has continued more or less into the early twenty-first century. The response in many of the world's largest film industries was to appeal to younger viewers, updating not only the content of films but also their scores. By the second half of the twentieth century, various forms of contemporaneous popular music could be heard in the cinemas of numerous national industries from India to Iran and from Mongolia to Mexico, where it was foregrounded as performance or utilized in the background score, and sometimes both.

In Bollywood, for instance, new genres such as the action film and crime film, and new musical influences such as rock 'n' roll, disco, and rap, were introduced. Rahul Dev ("R. D.") Burman mixed elements of disco and rock with the folk traditions of his native Bengal in his film scores such as *Sholay* (1975). Bollywood also accommodated its growing international audience. Although film songs have never disappeared from Hindi cinema, their prevalence diminished in films designed for export and their performance was incorporated in a more naturalistic way, as in *Lagaan: Once upon a Time in India* (2001), scored by A R. Rahman. It was nominated for an Oscar for Foreign Film in 2002.

Commercial pressures and consumer demand exerted themselves around the globe. In the Egyptian film industry, popular Egyptian music began to turn up in Egyptian film scores like those for Khairy Beshara's *Necklace and Bracelet* (1986), *Ice Cream in Glin* (1993), and *Abracadabra America* (1993). In Brazil, the score for Fernando Meirelles's *City of God* (2002) by Antonio Pinto and Ed Cortes mixes original composition with rap, soul, and disco. British, US, and Mexican rock and alt rock can be heard along with classical and contemporary Mexican pop music in Alfonso Cuarón's *Y tu mamá también* (2001) and US pop, reggae, and Cantonese covers of rock songs in *Chungking Express* (1994). In Mongolia, beginning in the 1970s, Anglo-American pop music including psychedelic rock and disco started to appear in films. In the post-Socialist era, when film production was no longer government-sponsored and was driven by a market economy, pop became the dominant musical mode, with Anglo-American, Cantonese, and Korean pop music, especially rock and hip-hop, filling soundtracks. The horror film *Khana* (2006) is scored for heavy metal. Even in the Soviet Union, rock 'n' roll appeared in soundtracks by the 1980s when limitations on artistic expression began to be lifted.

Hollywood, too, adopted popular music, especially rock 'n' roll, which would prove the most important new form of popular music in the second half of the twentieth century. By this point

Hollywood had already begun to diversify, acquiring record companies that allowed them to cross-promote their products through synergy: the recordings promoted the films and the films promoted the recordings. Rock 'n' roll was first heard briefly in *The Blackboard Jungle* (1955), where Bill Haley & His Comets performed "Rock Around the Clock" for the opening credits. Initially rock 'n' roll targeted the youth market, but Hollywood soon realized its potential. Rock infiltrated the background score in *Shaft* (1971), scored by Isaac Hayes, and in *Sorcerer* (1977) and *Risky Business* (1983), scored by Tangerine Dream. Some high-profile rock performers were lured to Hollywood to score film—Bob Dylan for *Pat Garrett & Billy the Kid* (1973), Eric Clapton for the *Lethal Weapon* franchise (1987–98), and Neil Young for *Dead Man* (1995). Rock would also prove a fertile seedbed for a generation of film composers: Peter Gabriel, Mark Knopfler, Danny Elfman, Ryuichi Sakamoto, Hans Zimmer, Jonny Greenwood, and Trent Reznor and Atticus Ross, among many others. But there was something even more radical than rock 'n' roll waiting in the wings that would change the very structure of the film score itself.

The compilation film score

The model that emerged in the second half of the twentieth century not only accommodated popular music, but also challenged conventional scoring practices that privileged original composition. The compilation score, as it has come to be known, developed in the 1970s and bears more than a passing resemblance to earlier bricolage models in Bollywood, China, Iran, and Egypt, the pastiche model of New German Cinema, the album-inspired Beatles films, the use of theme songs in Hollywood, and even the earliest musical accompaniments to silent film. Corey Creekmur has made the intriguing argument that Hollywood, in chasing the youth demographic, has gravitated closer and closer to a model for film scoring that Bollywood embraced in the 1930s.

Compilation scores consist of a series of songs, usually preexisting, occasionally originally composed, sometimes emanating from a source within the film but more often used as background music. The discreet musical pieces that make up the compilation score are typically derived from noncinematic sources (for example, opera or concert music, but most frequently popular music and especially rock 'n' roll), often used in their original recorded format and sometimes supplemented by original songs. The Beatles' phenomenally successful and highly influential films *A Hard Day's Night* (1964) and *Help!* (1965) are two precursors to the phenomenon. The compilation score for *American Graffiti* (1972) emanates from the local radio station that broadcasts the songs heard on car radios throughout the film. Compilation scores also can be combined with originally composed music, often orchestral, as is the case, for instance, in *The Shape of Water.*

Songs are different from instrumental music in several ways. On the one hand, songs can draw an audience's conscious attention more directly than background music and thus establish meaning more quickly and efficiently; songs have access to language, specifically lyrics, which can be a very explicit means of transmitting meaning. On the other hand, songs have a structure of their own and may not be as flexible or responsive as music composed expressly for a film. Because preexisting songs are more immediately recognizable, they also trail with them personal histories that trigger memories, experiences, and emotions that may be at odds with the film's dramatic needs. Still, songs are constituted through the language of music, and they utilize many of the same musical elements as the background score and often fulfill similar functions: providing unity, creating mood, heightening atmosphere, aiding characterization, establishing geographic space and time period, and connecting an audience emotionally to a film.

Compilation scores are often characterized by their eclecticism. Consider Wong Kar-wai's *Chungking Express* (1994), which includes Faye Wong's covers of "Dreams" by the Cranberries and "Bluebeard" by the Cocteau Twins; Dinah Washington's "What a Difference a Day Makes"; Dennis Brown's "Things in Life"; The Mamas & the Papas' "California Dreamin'"; and an original song, "Baroque," by Michael Galasso. The kaleidoscopic compilation score for Alfonso Cuarón's *Y tu mamá también* (2001) is composed entirely of source music and includes dozens of recordings by English- and Spanish-language performers: rockers Frank Zappa of the United States and Brian Eno of Britain, Australian singer Natalie Imbruglia, Spanish rap star La Mala (Rodriguez), the psychedelic 1970s Mexican rock band La Revolución de Emiliano Zapata, Mexican pop singer Edith Marquez, alternative Mexican rockers Café Tacuba, and legendary Sonoran guitarist and composer Ignacio Peñuñuri Jaime. Equally eclectic is the score for the New Zealand film *No. 2* (aka *Naming Number Two*) (2006), which features original scoring by Don McGhaslan alongside Pietro Mascagni's Intermezzo from *Cavalleria Rusticana*, Fijian traditional and popular music, Hawaiian steel guitar, Calypso, and New Zealand hip-hop, soul, and reggae.

Anahid Kassabian views the increased emphasis on song, especially in contemporary Hollywood film, as a positive and even liberating development. For Kassabian, the compilation score provides new possibilities for audiences to forge individual relationships to films and creates space for alternative voices, especially those of women and minorities, to be heard. Think of the ways in which the recordings of female singers on the soundtrack of *Thelma and Louise* (1991) give privileged insight into the protagonists' inner lives: Martha Reeves singing "Wild Night" or Tammy Wynette, "I Don't Wanna Play House." Baby, in *Baby Driver* (2017), is a getaway driver who suffers from tinnitus, a ringing in the ears. To drown out the distracting noise, Baby listens to music of his own choosing, through in-dash cassette players, record players, tape decks, jukeboxes, and, most frequently, earphones connected to an iPod. In doing so, Baby literally creates the soundtrack for the film. Those songs not only offer insight into Baby's psychic and emotional states, however; they also align with the dramatic needs of the narrative. In the opening six-minute bank heist and car chase, Baby turns on his iPod to hear Jon Spencer Blues Explosion's 1995 hit, "Bellbottoms," which drives both the cuts and the pace of the editing while giving the audience a window into Baby's personality. He is one cool cat. How the audience hears what Baby is listening to through earphones is not explained.

Or consider *Marie Antoinette* (2006), Sofia Coppola's postmodernist take on eighteenth-century French history, which plays fast and loose with chronology in the compilation score, from a Rameau aria, *"Tristes apprêts, pâles flambeaux,"* to Bow Wow Wow's "I Want Candy" in order to embody the director's vision both of Marie Antoinette and of history itself. Explains Coppola, "The film's candy colors, its atmosphere and teenaged music all reflect and are meant to evoke how I saw that world from Marie-Antoinette's perspective." Or marvel at Alfonso Cuarón's *Roma* (2018), where music from the compilation score, meticulously chosen from 1970s Mexican popular music, was selected to create different musical environments for each room in the house: the music in the children's room is very different from the music in the kitchen, which is very different from the music on the rooftop. According to music supervisor Lynn Fainchtein, the music for the film "was selected down to the most miniscule detail."

Indigenous music in the film score

The second half of the twentieth century was a tumultuous period for film and film music. National industries dealt with its challenges in different ways. In terms of music, Hollywood put Romanticism on the back burner, incorporated more popular music, and came to rely on the compilation score. Other national industries exploited popular music too, and in many of those industries indigenous music, both traditional and popular, came to the fore. In Latin America, the film industries of Mexico, Brazil, and Argentina faced stiff competition from cheap Hollywood imports, and filmmakers found themselves caught between the demands of commercial success and the commitment to uniquely national concerns. Many filmmakers, especially those with status as international auteurs, tried to do both as the scores for their films attest, combining elements of Hollywood scoring and/or European concert music with indigenous music. The films of Portuguese director João César Monteiro exemplify this trend in films such as *Recollections of the Yellow House* (1989), where Schubert songs share the soundtrack with popular music. In the documentaries of Brazilian filmmaker Glauber Rocha, such as *Barravento* (1962), *Black God, White Devil* (1964), and *Land in August* (1967), originally composed musical cues coexist with quotations from European concert music (Bach, Verdi), Brazilian concert music (Heitor Villa-Lobos), and Brazilian and Afro-Brazilian musics (the samba and the candomblé). In Paul Leduc's *Frida* (1984), Mexican corridos and Spanish zarzuela exist alongside European concert music (Saint-Saëns, Sibelius, Prokofiev). The score for Fernando Meirelles's *City of God* (2002) by Antonio Pinto and Ed Cortes mixes rap, soul, and disco with Brazilian samba.

Often indigenous music did more than share the soundtrack with concert music or Hollywood scoring. It provided a critique of those musical traditions, as in many of the films listed above. Some filmmakers used the musical score for even more trenchant political commentary. In Cuba, after the revolution, many films used music to challenge Hollywood and Latin American cinemas and to create a new national identity. The Grupo de Experimentación Sonora de ICAIC was formed to promote and revolutionize Cuban music, including film music. Grupo questioned rigid divisions between concert music and popular music and the use of genre conventions in film scoring. Their aesthetics can be heard in films of the 1960s (and beyond), such as *El Joven rebelde* (1961), *Lucía* (1968), and *79 Primaveras* (1969).

In Argentina, *Tangos! The Exile of Gardel* (1985) was scored by Astor Piazzolla with tangos, only two years after the fall of the military junta that had banned tangos in an attempt to destroy allegiance to Argentinean culture. Alberto Iglesias scored a number of films for Pedro Almodóvar, including *Pain and Glory* (2019), *Julieta* (2016), *The Skin I Live In* (2011), *Volver* (2006), *Bad Education* (2004), and *Talk to Her* (2002), often using indigenous Spanish music, like the bolero, and frequently set against Hollywood scoring.

Arab filmmakers continue the long tradition of using indigenous music, particularly popular song, in the film score. Lebanese singer Majida El-Roumi can be heard in Youssef Chahine's *The Return of the Prodigal Son* (1976), and performances of Arab song are interpolated into films such as Beshara's *Crabs* (1991) and Daoud Abd El-Sayyed's *al-Kitkat* (1991). Pop singers are featured, too. Muhammad Munir is heard in Beshara's *Necklace and Bracelet* (1986) and the pop stars Amr Diyab and Muhammad Fu-ad in Beshara's *Ice Cream in Glin* (1993) and *Abracadabra America* (1993). Assia Djebar's *The Nuba of the Women of Mont Chenoua* (1976) features nuba, traditional music originating in Arab Spain in the Middle Ages, as both the subject and the score. In Lebanon, *Bosta* (2005) incorporates indigenous music and dance juxtaposed against the disruptive force of European techno music. African filmmakers have traditionally relied on indigenous music and instruments. Two twenty-first-century examples that position indigenous music in particularly interesting ways are the Senegalese *Karmen Geï* (2001) and Guinean *Nha Fala* (2002). In both films, the performance of song serves as both a fusion of and a clash between traditional African music and Hollywood genre and scoring conventions.

Indigenous music, both operatic and popular, continued to provide a crucial component in the development of Chinese-language film industries outside China. In Hong Kong, in the Cantonese industry, films featuring Chinese opera continued as dependable audience pleasers well into the 1970s, and in the Mandarin industry, musicals tapped into indigenous popular music and dance. In Taiwan in the 1980s, the director Hou Hsiao-hsien began his career in a similar vein with a series of musicals starring pop singers Feng Fei-Fei and Kenny Bee and featuring numerous pop songs. In Korean cinema, Im Kwon-taek brought traditional Korean *p'ansori*, a kind of Korean folk opera, into popular Korean culture in *Sop'yonje* (1993) and *Chunhyang* (2000). Hong Kong films tapped into a vibrant pop music aesthetic in the 1980s, featuring recording stars in acting roles and loading films with contemporary pop songs. Even John Woo's police thriller, *The Killer* (1989), has three songs performed by Sally Yeh, the film's female lead. Following the British transfer to China in 1999, Chinese rock 'n' roll has informed a series of films steeped in techniques of cinema verité to capture post-socialist angst.

Indigenous popular song features importantly in recent Congolese filmmaking. In *Boma-Tervuren* (1999), the soundtrack fluctuates between Gregorian chant and indigenous musical elements. In *Lumumba: La mort du prophète* (1990), the Congolese popular song "Independence Cha-Cha" forms a crucial part of the soundtrack where, among other things, it accompanies scenes of Belgium on the image track, reversing the colonized/colonizer dichotomy with the colonial power, Belgium, colonized by Congolese music. In *Lamokowang* (2004), indigenous instruments and songs comprise the soundtrack, an aural marker of the importance of tradition.

Challenges

The Iranian film industry struggled in the 1950s and 1960s against competition from Bollywood and Hollywood film, and the Islamic Revolution dealt it a near-fatal blow in 1979. The new government officially condemned the West and imposed strict censorship, including banning Iranian films that were successful on the international film circuit from being shown in Iran. Iran's vibrant musical scene was curtailed, and composers and musicians found themselves out of work. Yet Hamid Naficy argues that it was these very conditions that "helped to create a new

'Islamic' cinema." Composers blocked from careers in the concert hall, such as Hossein Alizadeh, moved to film scoring, which provided a livelihood and increased access to audiences through popular recordings of film scores. By the 1980s, cinema became the most popular form of entertainment in Iran.

The scores of the Iranian New Wave reflect this refocus on national issues. Although many New Wave films hew to a neo-realist aesthetic and use music sparingly, some prominently feature music such as those of the Kurdish Iranian director Bahman Ghobadi, especially his musical trilogy, three films that revolve around musicians and feature numerous musical performances: *Marooned in Iraq* (2002), *Half Moon* (2006), and *No One Knows About Persian Cats* (2009). In *Half Moon*, scored by Alizadeh, a family of musicians, Kurdish exiles in Iran, return to Iraqi Kurdistan after the fall of Saddam Hussein to perform in a celebratory concert. The story provides plenty of opportunities for performances of Kurdish traditional and popular indigenous music, and the score features Persian instruments, some of which are viewed being made in the film. In Mohsen Makhmalbaf's *Gabbeh* (1996), Alizadeh's score gravitates to the otherworldly aspects of the narrative (the story concerns a love story told from the perspective of a woman whose spirit lives in a *gabbeh*, or Persian carpet), which are represented musically by unusual combinations of Persian and Western instruments.

The 1949 communist takeover of China, now officially the People's Republic of China, ushered in an era of state-financed and -controlled cinema, not unlike that under Joseph Stalin in the Soviet Union. After the vitality of the early sound-era scores, those in the first years of the People's Republic of China often seem conventional by comparison, with music used to supply mood and atmosphere. Production there slowed and by the 1970s had virtually ceased; the action had moved to Hong Kong, which would become the most prolific of the Chinese-language film industries. A low point came with Mao Tse-tung's Cultural Revolution, 1976–86, when traditional Chinese music and Western music of any kind were banned.

It was not until the Open Door Policy of the 1980s that the Chinese film industry recovered, with a new generation of filmmakers, dubbed the Fifth Generation, and a new breed of composers, the New Wave, leading the way. New Wave composers rose to prominence scoring these films. Many had studied in the West. Zhao Jiping is the most prominent among them, scoring several films for Zhang Yimou (*Red Sorghum* [1987], *Ju Dou* [1990], and *Raise the Red Lantern* [1991]) and for Chen Kaige (*Yellow Earth* [1984] and *Farewell My Concubine* [1993]), combining elements of traditional Chinese music with Western harmonies and instrumentation. For *Farewell My Concubine*, Zhao exploited Chinese opera and achieved some intriguing effects using its percussive instruments, which he electronically altered. These films were, however, not immune to government censorship, and many films that were successful internationally were not even screened in the People's Republic of China.

Tan Dun scores films with the same fusion of Chinese and Asian musical elements with Western forms and instrumentation that characterizes his concert work. An Oscar winner for his score for Ang Lee's *Crouching Tiger, Hidden Dragon* (2000), a US–Taiwan co-production, Tan combined ancient Chinese instruments, Chinese opera, Japanese kabuki musical traditions, a battery of Asian percussion, and a Western symphony orchestra with the world-famous cellist Yo-Yo Ma. Like Zhao Jiping, Tan Dun has experienced his share of criticism for banking on Western fantasies of China. As he explains it, however, he is promoting Chinese music as part of the international language of music: "I'm Marco Polo going backward from East to West."

World music and global influences

In use since the 1980s, the term *world music* is a fairly diffuse and loosely defined concept; it is a term devised in the Western world to refer to non-Western, indigenous traditional music. Put another

6. Tan Dun (left) won an Oscar in 2000 (Best Original Score) for his score for *Crouching Tiger, Hidden Dragon*, which prominently features solos by the cellist Yo-Yo Ma (right).

way, world music is what indigenous music is called when Hollywood uses it. World music became an increasingly audible component of film scoring in Hollywood starting in the late twentieth century, and it can turn up in some predictable but even some surprising places, for example, *qawwali*, Sufi Muslim devotional music originating in northern India, sung by the noted Pakistani singer Nusrat Fateh Ali Khan in *The Last Temptation of Christ* (1988) but also in *Dead Man Walking* (1995), a film about capital punishment set in prison.

Kecak, a form of Balinese Hindu dance music, turns up in the Coen Brothers' neo-noir *Blood Simple* (1984). Alberto Iglesias used Middle Eastern instruments including the *sarangi*, *bansuri*, *ney*, *santur*, *rubab*, and tabla, in his score for *The Kite Runner* (2007), set in Afghanistan. But North African *raï*, itself a veritable melting pot of worldwide influences and sung by *raï* star Khaled, can be heard in Eric Serra's score for *The Fifth Element* (1997), a sci-fi action film. The *duduk*, an Armenian wind instrument, turns up in Hans Zimmer and Lisa Gerrard's score for *Gladiator* (2000), set in ancient Rome, and a Native American flute and Sudanese gamelans appear in Mychael Danna's score for *The Ice Storm* (1997), set in contemporary Connecticut. Baby in *Baby Driver* listens to Egyptian reggae on his iPod.

It remains an open question whether world music in a film's soundtrack introduces audiences to music previously unavailable to them or exploits and commodifies a culture's indigenous music and represents yet another example of the West's co-opting of non-Western cultures for commercial gain. In an interesting twist on the use (or exploitation?) of indigenous music in Hollywood film (and a wry comment on its musical stereotyping of Asians), the compilation score of *Crazy Rich Asians* (2018) contains Chinese and Mandarin covers of Anglo-American pop songs, including Cold Play's "Yellow."

Film music has always, in a sense, been world music, and by that I mean that film music has been and continues to be a global enterprise. While many films are tied to their countries of origin by their sources of funding and their audiences (although even this is becoming less and less true), they have long been infused with global influences. That trail of globalization can be followed through the history of film music. The influx of composers from one country and culture to another, as well as the diffusion of the musical practices they bring with them, is a process that began long before the concept of globalization came into focus. Film music has always been transnational: European composers emigrating to Hollywood trailing Romanticism behind them; early sound film scores in China quoting Strauss waltzes as well as leftist revolutionary songs; production numbers in Egyptian films drawing from Latin American and African musical elements; *film Farsi* exploiting cues from Hollywood films alongside Persian music played on traditional Persian instruments; Hollywood influencing Bollywood and Bollywood influencing Hollywood. The production of scores has also become globalized. To create *Crouching Tiger, Hidden Dragon*, cellist Yo-Yo Ma, supervised by Tan Dun, recorded his solos in New York; they were later integrated with the orchestral score recorded in Shanghai with Tan conducting a Western symphony with traditional Chinese instruments and a battery of Asian percussion.

7. A. R. Rahman was a double Oscar winner for Best Original Song ("Jai Ho") and Best Original Score for *Slumdog Millionaire* (2008).

A. R. Rahman

Globalization is very apparent in the career of A. R. Rahman, born and raised in Madras (now Chennai) in India and educated at Oxford University in England. Rahman began his professional life as a musician writing jingles for television commercials. Credited with revolutionizing film scoring in his native India and catapulted into international prominence with his double Oscar win for score and song in *Slumdog Millionaire* (2008), Rahman stands at the forefront of the globalization of film scoring.

Rahman earned his first film commission in Kollywood for *Roja* (1992), scoring the film in an eclectic mix of Tamil folk and traditional music, reggae, African rhythms, lush violins and Romantic harmonies, and hints of Morricone's spaghetti western scores. Rahman later began scoring films in the Hindi industry, the first of which, the enormously popular *Rangeela* (1995), incorporated Bollywood disco beats. As his career has progressed, his music has absorbed a number of global influences. In addition to Tamil and Hindi folk and traditional music, reggae, African rhythms, and Morricone's spaghetti western film scores, there is *qawwali*, Sufi Islamic chanting, Asian music, Western concert music, and Western pop music, especially hip-hop, rap, disco, and technopop.

Rahman is the most successful film composer in India. His soundtrack albums have sold more copies than the Beatles. Globally, his work includes the West End/Broadway musical *Bombay Dreams* (2002) produced by Andrew Lloyd Webber; scores for English-language films such as *Elizabeth: The Golden Age* (2007) (with Craig Armstrong), *127 Hours* (2010), *People Like Us* (2012), and *Million Dollar Arm* (2014); the Mandarin-language film *Warriors of Heaven and Earth* (2003); and, of course, the English/Hindi-language film *Slumdog Millionaire*. When asked whether he believed in a universal music, he answered, "I do, because all of us are, in a way, getting multicultural in our ears."

Chapter 7
Composers and their craft

Film composers, those men and women who compose the original music we hear in the background of a film, have produced some of the most memorable and highly recognizable music in the twentieth and twenty-first centuries. Film composers hail from all walks of musical life: the concert hall (Dmitri Shostakovich, Sergei Prokofiev, Sofia Gubaidulina, Aaron Copland, Philip Glass, Hossein Alizadeh, Tôru Takemitsu, Tan Dun, Valentin Silvestrov); the opera house (Erich Wolfgang Korngold, Richard Hageman); Broadway (Max Steiner, Alfred Newman); radio (Bernard Herrmann); performance careers (Ravi Shankar, Miles Davis, Terence Blanchard, Hildur Guðnadóttir); television (Henry Mancini, Quincy Jones, Ramin Djawadi, Jon Batiste); advertising (A. R. Rahman); and rock music (Danny Elfman, Ryuichi Sakamoto, Jonny Greenwood, Mica Levi, and Trent Reznor and Atticus Ross). Some have come up the ranks through apprenticeships in film scoring. (Ramin Djawadi, John Powell).

Some composers have complained, sometimes bitterly, about the constraints of scoring film; others have found film scoring liberating. And for some, film composing was a refuge from political repression (Shostakovich) and in some cases may even have saved their lives (Korngold, Waxman, Prokofiev, and Shostakovich). Here thumbnail sketches of core issues and key processes involved in film composing are fleshed out with stories of individual film composers negotiating their craft.

Composing for films

The process of composing a film score depends on a number of factors: institutional practices (large studio systems such as Hollywood and Bollywood versus small-scale production) and the circulation of power within them (in Hollywood composers are part of an assembly line mode of production, but in Bollywood, music directors developed considerable freedom in the production of the score and many enjoy celebrity status); the relationships at work on a given film (longtime collaborations between directors and composers, for example, Steven Spielberg and John Williams); the power of the director and his or her interest in the musical score (Wong Kar-wai and Quentin Tarantino leap to mind here); and the individual personalities and proclivities of the composers themselves (such as the notoriously prickly Herrmann, who insisted, "I have the final say about my music; otherwise I refuse to do the music for the film"). Still, there is a core set of issues involved in film scoring that composers around the world negotiate.

Starting

Where and when to begin the process of composition is among the first decisions a film composer must make. Some composers prefer to read the script for inspiration. Gabriel Yared, for one, will not take on a project without seeing the script. In his collaborations with Jean-Jacques Beineix, Yared read and discussed the scripts with Beineix and met with the actors in preproduction. Yared's scores were largely complete before filming began so that Beineix could play Yared's music on the set. Takemitsu would read a script before taking a job and wanted to be brought into the production as early as possible, often visiting the set during filming. Elfman likes to visit the set during production, too, and has credited seeing the *Batman* (1989) set as the inspiration for the score's theme. Liu Zhuang would read the script and go on location to get a feel for the material. For *Border Town* (1984), she visited West Hunan and researched local folk music, which she was able to incorporate into the score. And Dun claims that he and director Ang Lee began their discussions about the score for *Crouching Tiger, Hidden Dragon* (2000) four years before production began.

These are exceptional experiences, however. Standard operating procedure around the world is to bring the composer in after the film has been shot. (Animation works in reverse: composers create the score before animators begin their work, allowing intricate effects in the coordination of music and image.) Many composers prefer it this way. Steiner quipped, "I never read a script. I run a mile when I see one." Herrmann claimed that he "could never work from a script when scoring a Hitchcock film.... You can't guess his musical requirements ahead of time." Although she reads the scripts, Zhuang waits until the editing is complete to begin scoring: "But you know, even though a script [says] there should be music here or here or here, that always changes as the film is in progress."

And as Maurice Jarre found out the hard way, composing ahead of time does not always work out. Jarre completed his score for *The Mosquito Coast* (1986) in advance of production so that director Peter Weir could play it on the set. And Weir did play Jarre's score during shooting; it was just not the one ultimately heard in the completed film. Weir's conception of the music changed dramatically during filming, and Jarre had to produce an entirely new score.

Still, some composers swear by working from a script, like Philip Glass. He compares film scoring to composing an opera, where he always works from a libretto: "The only way for music to become an organic part of the film [is] to begin with the script."

Spotting the film

Most composers will see the film for the first time in rough cut, an initial and provisional edit of the film. This allows composers to respond to what actually ends up on film but also puts them under tremendous time constraints. In the Hollywood studio system, composers were given a window of roughly three to six weeks, although certain composers, such as Korngold, had the prestige and thus the power to demand more time. That time frame has not changed substantially in the early twenty-first century. Ennio Morricone would ask for one month. Rahman finished the score for *Slumdog Millionaire* (2008) in three weeks. The eight months that Yared had to compose the score for *Possession* (2002) was possible only because Yared scored the film before he had the opportunity to see any of it.

For most composers, scoring begins with spotting the film, that is, screening the rough cut and deciding which spots need music and how much. Says John Barry, "The choices about where the music goes in a movie are the most important decisions you can make." He adds, "Ninety percent of the time those choices are really very clear and both the director and yourself are in sync." In general the task of spotting falls to the director, composer, and music editor, who make these determinations depending on the power of the director (or the extent to which he or she is invested in the score), the composer's ability to assert his or her choices (as Morricone so delicately put it, "sometimes...the director tends to assert himself...to the detriment of the authority of the composer"), and the nature of the relationships among the participants.

In Bollywood, spotting (referred to as marking) is the domain of the music department. On *Slumdog Millionaire*, director Danny Boyle spotted the film himself. Rahman, one of the most prolific film composers in the world, was used to working in Bollywood, where the composer makes all those decisions. On trusting the director to do the marking, Rahman commented, "It was a totally different way of working." Still, says Rahman, who won two Oscars for the film, "it worked out all right."

Collaborating

In the early twenty-first century, the director is a key figure in the creation of an original score; it is his or her vision, typically, that the composer works to realize. Collaborating with the director can give the composer an active role in the filmmaking process, and many directors today acknowledge the importance of working directly with the composer. Paul Thomas Anderson, who has collaborated with Jonny Greenwood on four films said, "To make a film, the final big collaborator that you have is the composer." And of Greenwood, "It's one of the great joys of my life— collaborating with him." On *There Will Be Blood* (2007), their first collaboration, Greenwood provided a cue before Anderson started shooting and which Anderson played on set. It ended up the opening track of the film. By *Inherent Vice* (2014), Greenwood had become essential. "He's always the first viewer, too." For *The Phantom Thread*, Anderson contacted Greenwood as soon as he saw the script.

The collaboration between Sergei Eisenstein and Sergei Prokofiev is legendary. On *Alexander Nevsky* (1938), Eisenstein involved Prokofiev from the beginning of the project. Prokofiev visited the set and regularly watched the dailies. According to Eisenstein, the two men would "bargain long and earnestly over 'which is to be the first'" and fought it out over whether it should be the music or the image. Sometimes Eisenstein won: Prokofiev would watch Eisenstein's edited footage and score to the completed footage. Sometimes Prokofiev won: some of the score was composed and recorded before the film was shot, enabling Eisenstein to shoot and edit some sequences to the score.

Important director–composer collaborations across film history include Jean Vigo and Maurice Jaubert, Jean Cocteau and Georges Auric, Claude Chabrol and Pierre Jansen, and Jacques Demy and Michel LeGrande in France; Grigori Kozintsev and Dmitri Shostakovich in the Soviet Union; Kenji Mizoguchi and Fumio

Hayasaka and Hayao Miyazaki and Joe Hisaishi in Japan; Jiří Trnka and Václav Trojan in Czechoslovakia; Federico Fellini and Nino Rota and Leone and Morricone in Italy; Fassbinder and Peer Raben and Werner Herzog and Popol Vuh in Germany; Pedro Almodovar and Alberto Iglesias in Spain; and Zhang Yimou and Zhao Jiping in China. The Hollywood studio system was not conducive to director–composer collaborations. But in the early twenty-first century, there are many such ongoing collaborations in Hollywood, including Steven Spielberg and John Williams, Spike Lee and Terence Blanchard, Tim Burton and Danny Elfman; Joel and Ethan Coen and Carter Burwell; Christopher Nolan and Hans Zimmer; and Wes Anderson and Alexandre Desplat.

The extent of collaboration between director and composer has varied tremendously depending on institutional practice, the power and personality of a particular director, and the influence of a particular composer. Some directors have composed the score themselves: D. W. Griffith composed the love theme for his *The Birth of a Nation* (1915), and Teinosuke Kinugasa composed the score when his avant-garde *A Page of Madness* (1927) was rediscovered and reissued in the 1970s. Other directors who have assumed the composer role themselves include Charlie Chaplin, John Carpenter, and Clint Eastwood.

Satyajit Ray is probably the director with the most extensive resume of film scores, composing many for his own films and several for other directors. Ray's relationships with the composers of his earliest films, Ravi Shankar, Ali Akbar Khan, and Ustad Vilayat Khan, were strained at best, and Shankar, in particular, bristled at what he considered Ray's increasing interference. Ray had an extensive knowledge and appreciation of Western music and wanted to use it in his films. He would claim that forms of Western concert music like the sonata influenced the very structure of his films and that Indian music, with its unfixed sense of time, chafed against the very construction of cinema itself. Discussions with his composers were proving fruitless, and

Composers and their craft

eventually Ray found it easier to score his films himself. He would begin by conceiving the key musical ideas as he wrote the screenplay—often whistling tunes before he wrote them down—and then developing those tunes throughout production.

Other directors have little interest in collaboration and very specific ideas about the music, tangling with composers as a result. Kurosawa gave his composers musical models to imitate: Ravel's *Bolero* for *Rashomon* (1950), Lizst's *Second Hungarian Rhapsody* for *Yojimbo* (1961) and *Sanjuro* (1962), Haydn's Symphony 101 (*The Clock*), and Beethoven's Ninth Symphony for *Red Beard* (1965). Akira Ifukube, who scored *The Quiet Duel* (1949), felt so compromised by the experience that he would not work for Kurosawa again. Fumio Hayasaka, whose untimely death devastated Kurosawa, fought with the director over the use of Ravel's *Bolero* as a musical prototype for *Rashomon*. He lost. Still, Hayakawa managed to sustain a working relationship with Kurosawa over the course of several films.

Japan's most celebrated composer of concert music, Takemitsu was used to directors ceding control to him. For *Dodeskaden* (1970), however, Kurosawa wanted Takemitsu to copy Bizet's *L'Arlésienne*. Takemitsu responded that if Kurosawa wanted Bizet, he should hire Bizet. Kurosawa, perhaps stunned by such unexpected insubordination, let Takemitsu compose original music instead. For *Ran* (1985), Kurosawa wanted Mahler's First Symphony. Takemitsu objected but found a workaround, using Mahler's *Songs of the Earth* instead. If Kurosawa noticed Takemitsu's disobedience, he never said anything about it. Eventually, however, Takemitsu had enough and walked away from *Rhapsody in August* (1991) after decades of what he felt was Kurosawa's unwelcome interference.

Some directors have, shall we say, interesting ideas about how music should be used in their films. Jean-Luc Godard, among film's most iconoclastic directors, asked Michel Legrand to write a theme and variations for *Vivre sa vie* (1962) and then used only one of the twelve variations, truncating its use by abruptly halting the music in mid-variation, including at the end of the film. The process between Pablo Larrain and Mica Levi on *Jackie* (2016) was similarly unconventional. Levi composed musical cues to fit specific scenes, which Larrain then reassigned to completely different scenes. "I think she was a little perplexed by that at first.... but that's how the score developed."

And then there are the failed collaborations. There is no more notorious example than the "collaboration" between Stanley Kubrick and Alex North for *2001: A Space Odyssey* (1968). Kubrick culled a series of selections from his record collection, including Richard Strauss's *Also Sprach Zarathustra*, as a temp track, a set of musical cues culled from existing music used as a temporary score for the rough cut until the original score is completed. Kubrick agreed to hire North to compose an original score. Kubrick and North spotted the film together and Kubrick played North the temp track, but then Kubrick and North had no further communication. According to North, "He told me to go off on my own." Kubrick decided that he liked his temp track better than North's contemporary score, and without so much as a word to North, he discarded North's entire score—which North discovered at the film's premiere. According to North, "It was the most frustrating experience of my entire career." It remains, along with *Torn Curtain*, Herrmann's score discarded by Hitchcock, one of cinema's great lost opportunities.

But it is not the only one. The practice of discarding completed scores continues in the twenty-first century. Recent scores jettisoned by directors after completion include Elmer Bernstein's *Gangs of New York*, Mychael Danna's *The Hulk* (2003), and Jóhann Jóhannsson's *Blade Runner 2049* (2017), to name just a few. Original scores of films made internationally are particularly vulnerable and often replaced by the film's distributor for US release out of fears that they are unmarketable. Eric Serra's score for the French film *Le Grand Bleu* (1988) was replaced with a score by Bill Conti and Angel Peña's score for the Puerto Rican English-language film *The Disappearance of Garcia Lorca* (1997) was replaced with one by Mark McKenzie. The Japanese film *Koneko monogatari* (1989) was originally scored by Ryuichi Sakamoto but went through three different replacement scores before Columbia Pictures settled on one by Michael Boddicker. For the Hungarian film *A játékos* (1997), the original score by Gerard Schurmann was replaced with one by Brian Lock. For *Tsotsi* (2005), a South African film, the replacement score was re-replaced with the original by Paul Hepker and Mark Kilian.

Institutional practices also limit collaboration between composers and directors. Certain film industries developed music formulas that were considered integral to success. Hindi cinema, *film Farsi*, Hong Kong cinema, Egyptian cinema, and Nigerian cinema require certain kinds and amounts of music. It may be difficult, if not impossible, for directors or composers to circumvent these expectations. And commercial pressure to include a pop song to

8. Composer John Barry (right) and director Kevin Costner (middle) at a scoring session for *Dances with Wolves* (1990). Said Costner of working with Barry: "We're not exactly sharing the same vocabulary...[but] he understands exactly what I mean."

appeal to certain audience demographics and sell the score as a soundtrack album is a global phenomenon. Morricone described being "pressed" to produce a score "as appealing as possible—melodic, easy, so that the majority of the audience likes it."

The Hollywood studio system, which privileged management over labor, famously curtailed collaboration. Authority over the score could be seized at any moment by the music department head, the film's producer, or even the studio chief. Miklós Rózsa remembers a producer who decreed that "the heroine's music was to be in a major key, the hero's in the minor, and that when the two were together, the music should be both major and minor." On *Spellbound* (1945), Rózsa asserts that he only saw Hitchcock twice but was "bombarded by the famous Selznick memos, which virtually told me how to compose and orchestrate the music scene by scene," instructions that Rózsa "completely disregarded."

Bernard Herrmann and Alfred Hitchcock: a collaboration

A director-composer collaboration that was uncharacteristically engendered and sustained within the Hollywood studio system was that between Alfred Hitchcock and Bernard Herrmann. Herrmann once declared, "If you were to follow the taste of most directors, the music would be awful. They really have no taste at all. I'm overstating a bit, of course. There are exceptions.... Hitchcock is very sensitive: he leaves me alone!" Hitchcock had definite ideas about the music and a good intuitive sense of where it should go, often reflected in detailed sound notes. He did not leave Herrmann alone, although he gave him plenty of room and came to depend on him. For the famous love scene in *Vertigo* (1958), when Judy emerges in the hotel room as Scotty's fantasy, an extended sequence with no dialogue, Hitchcock explained to Herrmann, "We'll just have the camera and you."

(continued)

Herrmann was involved from the beginning and attended preproduction meetings with Hitchcock, came and went on the set, offered suggestions not only about the score but also about other aspects of the film, was consulted about the placement of music, and even disregarded Hitchcock's directives when he disagreed with them. On *Psycho* (1960), Hitchcock determined that the shower sequence did not need music. Herrmann thought otherwise, producing one of the most arresting (and imitated) music cues in all of cinema, which Hitchcock, to his credit, immediately recognized when he first heard it.

As the partnership continued, however, it began to sour and finally ended badly. Hitchcock was under pressure from the studio to use pop music in *Torn Curtain* (1966). Herrmann refused to have anything to do with such commercial pressures. He was fired unceremoniously by Hitchcock after recording one cue of his completed score. Hitchcock would later dump the score that Henry Mancini composed for *Frenzy* (1972), because, as he told Mancini, it sounded too much like Herrmann. Once friends on set and off, Hitchcock and Herrmann never reconciled. Hitchcock credited Herrmann's music with 33 percent of the effect of *Psycho*. Herrmann revised that figure upward to 60 percent. What is not in dispute is Herrmann's ability to give musical form to the unconscious fears and desires at the heart of Hitchcock, in films such as *The Man Who Knew Too Much* (1956), *Vertigo*, *North by Northwest* (1959), and, of course, *Psycho*.

Composing

The most indefinable part of film scoring comes next: composing. Film composers have a variety of explanations for how they find inspiration (or how they function when they do not), and they range from bolt-out-of-the-blue flashes of inspiration to disciplined craftsmanship. Anil Biswas, working in Bollywood in the 1930s, said, "Music must belong to the period and to the character [of the film], and that used to give me ideas when I sat to compose." Rachel Portman describes her experience in this way: "It can be something very small, like a four-note melodic chain or a movement from one chord to another, that you suddenly know is going to be the heart of the music, the language and the syntax for the entire film." Georges Delerue describes his experience in quite another: "In reality you have to force yourself, you have to concentrate on things like a sportsman does. That's when the ideas arrive." Says Jerry Goldsmith, "We like to think it is all art, but let's face it, we have to rely on craft a lot of times." Morricone, who by his own count composed more than 450 film scores, describes the process as part technique, part inspiration. Philip Glass cautions against becoming too immersed in the film: "Composers want to know how to write music, how you get an idea, and I tell them—and they are a little surprised—don't look at the movie too much." It sounds like that is what Ramin Djawadi does: "I usually start writing my themes without even writing to picture, just trying to find the tone."

Federico Fellini claimed he had an active hand in creating scores with longtime collaborator Nino Rota, describing how he would stand over Rota at the piano and tell him exactly what kind of music he wanted. Rota, however, tells the story a bit differently. A quick study and an exceptionally gifted improviser, Rota would compose multiple themes of his own ahead of time and play them for Fellini until he hit on one that Fellini liked, giving Fellini the impression that he was inspiring Rota at the piano.

Composers may work at a desk, at a piano, or, nowadays, at a computer keyboard. Aaron Copland composed at a piano while the film was projected. Some, like Morricone, composed conventionally with staff paper and a pencil; others, like Rahman, compose at a computer keyboard. Djawadi used to employ pencil and paper, but now he just sings into his cell phone. Some work in complete isolation, and some like hubbub. They are all under the gun to produce music quickly.

Orchestrating

Composers are largely able to complete their jobs, at least in large-scale production systems such as Hollywood and Bollywood, because of a highly specific division of labor. In Hollywood, from the studio era to the present, composers generally sketch out their ideas, in varying degrees of specificity, and work with orchestrators (and sometimes arrangers) who produce the final version of the score. This means that Hollywood composers rarely orchestrate their own music. In the international film music community, however, composers tend to orchestrate their own work and as a result can have trouble adjusting to working in Hollywood.

In Bollywood, before the advent of computer-driven score production in the 1990s, music directors would assemble teams for orchestrating, copying, conducting, and even composing the background score. In fact, before the end of the twentieth century, those who composed the background score often went uncredited, and thus it was assumed, wrongly, that music directors were responsible for all the music in a film, not just the songs. There were even actual assembly lines to produce scores. Benny Rosario remembers the process: "Vincent would mark the film, and then Anil would write something for the first mark, and Vincent would copy it, and then Anil would record it, and while he was recording, Arun would be writing something for the next mark, and again Vincent would copy, and then Arun would record, and Anil would be writing something. We never stopped." This meant keeping players at the ready throughout the scoring process, and composers established relationships with players they could depend on to participate in this way.

Composers, especially those working in Hollywood, have learned to compensate for the fact that film scores are not produced by a single individual. Many composers create an elaborate sketch including not only melody and harmony but also orchestration cues. John Barry, for instance, writes extremely detailed sketches on a twelve-stave score with harmonies and instrumentations, including all the solo parts, written out. Others, like James Horner, will fully orchestrate a few bars and leave the orchestrator to finish the cue. Still others establish a long-term relationship with an orchestrator or arranger who could be trusted to reproduce a composer's style: Korngold with Hugo Friedhofer (who became an important composer himself), Dimitri Tiomkin with choral arranger Jester Hairston, John Williams with Herbert Spencer, Elfman with fellow Oingo Boingo band member Steve Bartek.

The relationship of Elfman and Bartek illustrates some of the anxieties that still surround orchestration in Hollywood. Elfman and Bartek were members of the eclectic rock band Oingo Boingo, but when Elfman first began film scoring in the 1980s, he composed in the Romantic, symphonic style of the classical Hollywood film score. His *Batman* (1989) is clearly modeled after scores of Korngold and Rózsa, Elfman's acknowledged influences. To this day, very few of Elfman's scores use pop music in any sustained way, and he has gone on record to express his dislike for pop scores.

Elfman has been completely candid about the contribution of Bartek. "I can write a fairly elaborate sketch—twelve, fourteen, or sixteen staves of music—but I depend on my orchestrator, Steve Bartek, to put it into a legitimate context." Bartek confirms that Elfman "writes every note in the score," although he did not exactly clarify things when he went on to describe Elfman's quirky musical notation: "He considers notation a problem for him, because [of]...dynamic markings....He's not good at bass clef...His notation is not strictly normal, but for anybody who knows anything about notation, you can look at it and figure out what he's saying." Elfman has been saddled for years with the (mis) perception that he is a hummer, in industry parlance, someone who cannot actually write music, much less orchestrate, and who hums the melodies to others who realize the score. Janet Halfyard argues that Elfman's experience in Hollywood unmasks deeply buried prejudices in the musical community against film scoring, holding film composers up to standards of the concert hall still steeped in Romantic notions of the inviolate individual creativity of the artist and his or her unique production of a work of art.

Recording and mixing

Many composers like to conduct the recording of their own scores and some are in a position to do so. In what might be called acoustic scores, it is the job of the conductor to precisely synchronize the music, conducted live, and the image track, usually projected on a large screen behind the orchestra and visible to the conductor. The lag time in perception between seeing an image and responding to it spurred the development of systems capable of assisting conductors and players in producing precise timing: the click track, an audible metronome delivered to the musicians via earphones, is still in use in the early twenty-first century. In the heyday of Hollywood, studios had large orchestras, anywhere from thirty-eight to sixty-five players under contract. Today, studios no longer have the luxury of keeping musicians on staff, but big-budget films can still command a huge orchestra: the score for *Batman* was recorded by 110 players, the score for *Dances with Wolves*, by ninety-five. In Bollywood, there were reportedly 300 musicians in the studio for *Mela* (1999)!

Not all recording sessions are devoted to recording a fully notated score, and music for film can be produced in other ways. The score for *Pather Panchali* (1955) was improvised by Ravi Shankar and a small group of musicians while watching the film in a recording studio. Ray remembers it took eleven hours; Shankar remembers it as four and a half. Shankar had not even seen all of the film when the recording session was held. Louis Malle asked Miles Davis to score *Elevator to the Gallows* (1958), giving Davis one night in the studio to improvise a score to a series of sequences that Malle had preselected. Alejandro Iñárritu asked Antonio Sánchez, a jazz drummer, to improvise a score, entirely for percussion, for *Birdman* (2018), which Sanchez did in a Los Angeles recording studio.

Not all scores are even recorded by acoustic instruments. Sampling can reproduce the sound of an acoustic instrument digitally, creating virtual instruments. Danny Elfman's MasterClass website includes samples from his digital library, including woodwinds and percussion, brass, strings, general orchestral, and native instruments. Sampling can also create original and unique musical sounds. Often used in horror films and in suspenseful scenes across genres, sampling can produce eerie and menacing effects. According to Elfman, what is difficult is producing "warmth and beauty" through sampling. Elfman's tip: "Grounding a synthesizer score with a piano is a good way to create an emotional connection to the viewer." Marco Beltrami had a severely restricted budget for *A Quiet Place* (2018), a horror/sci fi film where the protagonists live in silence to protect themselves from creatures who track their victims through sound. To provide emotional resonance, Beltrami planned on a full orchestra, but because of cost constraints ended up using a small ensemble of acoustic instruments mixed with synthesized sounds. For the family, however, Beltrami used acoustic strings and a detuned piano. The monsters got the synthesized mix.

The final stages of a score's production are mixing (adjusting sound levels after recording) and dubbing (adding all the various sound tracks, including the music track, to the edited film), processes in which the composer usually is not involved. If a cue is eliminated, the dubbing stage is most likely where it will happen. Cues often end up on the cutting room floor unbeknownst to the composer. "I try and stay fairly calm about cues disappearing under cars," says James Newton Howard. "What are you going to do?" Leonard Bernstein remembers attending a dubbing session for *On the Waterfront* (1954) and watching in horror as a music cue that he felt was crucial to the film was virtually eliminated to accommodate Marlon Brando's grunt.

The advent of technological innovations in sound production has had radical (some might argue liberating) consequences for film scoring and recording. It is theoretically possible now for composers to virtually create and produce an entire score on computer in a small studio space, eliminating the need for a traditional studio with all its resources. In fact, in many film industries composers now need computer expertise. Rahman had a transformative influence on film scoring in Bollywood, introducing computer composition (he still uses a Mac), sophisticated software, digital sampling, and synthesized film scores. It has now become so commonplace for scores to be digitally produced on a synthesizer in Bollywood that the very nomenclature has begun to change, with the term "programmer" replacing "music director" and the label New Bollywood registering these dramatic changes to film scoring.

Equally impactful (and not unrelated) has been the breakdown of studio systems and large music departments capable of handling all aspects of a score's production in some of the world's largest film industries, Bollywood and Hollywood. Composers became free agents, no longer in the full-time employ of a studio and often without its resources. With the advent of the synthesized score, some composers have been able to produce an entire film score from their own computer. Others have stepped up to fill the void in another way, creating their own music studios, an interesting twist on outsourcing.

The new studio system

Hans Zimmer's production company, Remote Control, has state-of-the-art music facilities on a sprawling campus that operates something like the music departments in the Hollywood studio system (or a medieval craft guild). Zimmer has everything in-house to create a film score, from pre- to postproduction, and he has been diligent about mentoring young composers, giving them the opportunity to train on the job, orchestrating, arranging, and even composing additional music for Zimmer's commissions. Zimmer served as the music producer of *Pirates of the Caribbean: The Curse of the Black Pearl* (2003), with screen credit for the score going to Klaus Badelt, a Zimmer protégé, and fifteen other composers working at Zimmer's studio getting "additional music by" credit. Many of these composers have gone on to major careers in film and television: Lisa Gerrard, Henry Jackman, Rupert Gregson-Williams, Ramin Djawadi, John Powell, Marc Streitenfeld, Steve Jablonsky, Mark Mancina, Steven Price, and Badelt, among others. Zimmer has credited his own mentors as the inspiration for his studio, among them Stanley Myers and Shirley Walker.

Separating composers from their craft

Sometimes composers have been prevented from practicing their craft by political events—world wars, civil wars, politics, cultural revolutions—and the attendant intellectual and artistic repression. Maurice Jaubert lost his life in the defense of Paris in 1940. Korngold acknowledged that *The Adventures of Robin Hood* saved his life. Korngold, who was Jewish, relocated to Hollywood in early 1938 to score the film for Warner Bros., but left his family behind in Vienna. When they were trapped by the Anschluss, the studio used its resources to help get them out of Austria. Korngold was convinced that had he not scored *Robin Hood*, he and his family would have perished in Nazi concentration camps. Franz Waxman, also Jewish, was severely beaten on the street by Nazi sympathizers in Berlin. Hanns Eisler, Bronislau Kaper, and Mario Castelnuovo-Tedesco all faced Nazi anti-Semitic laws that banned performance of their music. Richard Hageman, who was not Jewish, nevertheless saw his opera banned in Germany by the Nazis and all performances canceled. Rózsa was working in

London when the German blitzkrieg started and film production stopped. They all wound up in Hollywood.

The score for *Alexander Nevsky* did something close to saving Sergei Prokofiev's life in the Stalinist Soviet Union of the 1930s when artists, intellectuals, filmmakers, and composers feared for their lives (and many lost theirs, like Boris Shumyatsky, head of the Mosfilm film studio) when their ideas or their art did not pass muster with Soviet authorities. Prokofiev was under suspicion not only because he had been living in the West when he repatriated to Russia but also because he employed modernism, which, it was alleged, rendered his music inaccessible to the masses. He was charged with formalism and his music was banned from the concert hall. He turned to film scoring, including *Alexander Nevsky* (1938). When Stalin attended a preview, the film won his approval, protecting Prokofiev, at least for the time being, from the fate that had befallen others who strayed from the party line. Dmitri Shostakovich also found himself denounced as a formalist and his concert music banned. He kept a suitcase packed next to his door in case of arrest by Soviet authorities. He contemplated suicide and began sleeping in the stairwell. Shostakovich ultimately found refuge in scoring films and sustained a long career collaborating with Grigori Kozintsev from *The New Babylon* (1929) to *Hamlet* (1964) and *King Lear* (1971), often producing scores tinged with the very modernism that was forbidden in the concert hall.

During the Cultural Revolution in China, Western music was banned, as was traditional Chinese music of any kind, including opera and folk music. Tan Dun found himself reassigned from music school in Beijing to a rice paddy in Hunan for two years. The Islamic Revolution in Iran initially cast a dark shadow over the lives of many Iranian composers who were effectively prevented from pursuing careers in the concert hall by prohibitions on public performances of their music. Many, like Hossein Alizadeh, turned to film composing.

The world has been a volatile place and unfortunately continues to be so. As of this writing in 2022, Ukrainian artists, like other Ukrainians, have been forced to flee their homeland or endure horrific conditions resulting from the brutal and unprovoked attacks of Russia. Valentin Silvestrov, who has composed numerous film scores as well as concert music, escaped to Berlin with his daughter and granddaughter: "Both are young. They have to live!" Comparing Putin's invasion to the 2014 Maidan pro-democracy revolution, Silvestrov says, "Young people were killed there, both Russians and Ukrainians, all unarmed. And now the whole of Ukraine and the whole world is turning into the Maidan. Maidan was a chamber version, a kind of trio or duet. And now it's an orchestral version." We like to think of music as somehow untouched by politics, a pure form of artistic expression, unencumbered and unfettered by worldly concerns. But as film composers' lives demonstrate, worldly concerns can indeed separate a composer from his or her craft.

Film composers in the twenty-first century

Film composing in Hollywood has tended to be something of a closed shop, especially for women and people of color. Happily, there have been some significant changes in this situation in the twenty-first century when composers from groups that have traditionally lacked access have begun to emerge. African American composers such as Quincy Jones and Terence Blanchard established bodies of work before the twenty-first century and some prominent jazz artists such as Duke Ellington and Charles Mingus have scored films, but it is only recently that African American composers have come to the fore, scoring some very high-profile titles. Kris Bowers scored *Green Book* (2019), *The United States vs. Billie Holiday* (2020), and *King Richard* (2021). Michael Abels scored *Get Out* (2017), *Us* (2019), and *Nope* (2022). Mervyn Warren scored *A Raisin in the Sun* (2013) and *Mary J Blige's My Life* (2021). And in 2020, for the first time in Oscar history, two African American composers were nominated

x

Composers and their craft

113

for Original Score in the same year, Terence Blanchard for *One Night in Miami* (2020) and Jon Batiste, who won an Oscar for his first score, sharing the award with Trent Reznor and Atticus Ross for the animated feature *Soul* (2020). (Batiste wrote the jazz score for the gritty New York sections of the film and Reznor and Ross the music for the cosmic realm.) Still, I would point out that this access has largely been limited to films dealing with African American characters or subject matter. There is a long way to go.

The numbers remain daunting for women in Hollywood. Although Elizabeth Firestone and Ann Ronell found limited work in the studio era; Bebe Barron cowrote the first electronic score with her husband, Louis; Wendy Carlos innovated with synthesized scores; Shirley Walker scored blockbusters in the 1990s and 2000s; and Rachel Portman, Anne Dudley, and Hildur Guðnadóttir won Oscars for Original Score, women have been vastly underrepresented in Hollywood film scoring.

Prejudice abounds. In 2000 Hans Zimmer brought in Lisa Gerrard to work on *Gladiator*, only to be greeted by a storm of protest from the "boys club": "What are you doing? This is crazy, why a woman's voice in this movie?" (And for the record, Gerrard scored the bloodbath at Carthage and the crucifixions, among other grisly sequences.) Her contribution proved so central that Zimmer shared screen credit with her, but because of the byzantine peculiarities of the Academy's rules, her name was not included on the nomination for Original Score.

Progress has been slow. A 2018 study at the University of Southern California found that of the top one hundred fictional Hollywood films at the box office from 2007 to 2017, out of more than one thousand films, only sixteen were scored by women. A 2019 study from the Center for the Study of Women in Television & Film revealed that ninety-four percent of US films in 2018 were scored by men. And when Hildur Guðnadóttir won the Oscar for her score for *Joker* (2019), it was only the third time in Oscar history that a female composer won. And yet, according to Laura Karpman, herself a veteran of television, documentary, and film scoring, "The numbers are bleak, but the landscape isn't."

In the twenty-first century, that landscape is changing. Women are becoming increasingly prominent in US indie films and documentaries, even scoring some Hollywood blockbusters. Pinar Toprak scored *Captain Marvel* (2019), the first Marvel film scored by a woman, and *Lost City* (2022). Guðnadóttir scored *Joker* (2020) and *Tar* (2022). Many come from outside the United States. Toprak is Turkish. Guðnadóttir is Icelandic. Eímear Noone, who is Irish, scored *Two by Two: Overboard* (2020), *It's Dark Here* (2013), and *The Donner Party* (2009), and in 2020 was the first female conductor of the Oscar telecast. Sofia Gubaidulina, who is Russian, provided the music for *The Killing of a Sacred Deer* (2017). Lesley Barber, who is Canadian, scored *Manchester by the Sea* (2016) and *Late Night* (2019). Isobel Waller-Bridge, who scored *Emma* (2020), *Munich: The Edge of War* (2021), and *The Phantom of the Open* (2021), and Mica Levi, who scored *Under the Skin* (2013) and *Jackie* (2016), are British.

Women of color are also finding space in the US film industry. Germaine Franco, the first Latina composer admitted to the Academy of Motion Picture Arts and Sciences and the first woman to score a Disney animated feature, scored *Encanto* (2021). Melissa Hui, who is Chinese Canadian, scored the documentary *The First Movie* (2002). Kathryn Bostic, the first African American female composer admitted to the Academy, has scored several documentaries, including *Toni Morrison: The Pieces I Am* (2019), *Rita Moreno: Just a Girl Who Decided to Go for It* (2021), and *Amy Tan: An Unintended Memoir* (2021). Tamar-kali, who identifies as Afro-indigenous, scored *Mudbound* (2017) and *Shirley* (2020). And Amanda (Dolores Patricia) Jones, an Emmy-nominated television composer, scored the documentary films *Ringside* (2019), *Definition Please* (2020), and *Dreamland: The Burning of Black Wall Street* (2022).

The situation globally is more difficult to assess. Film composers who live and work internationally, when their resumes include a prominent Hollywood title or two, are fairly easy to find, such as Guðnadóttir, Noone, Levi, and Waller-Bridge. Also visible are Ramin Djawadi, an Iranian German who lives in Berlin, who scored the high-profile *Game of Thrones* (2011–19) and has built a reputation in big-budget Hollywood films like *Iron Man* (2008), *Pacific Rim* (2013), and *A Wrinkle in Time* (2018); Jóhann Johannsson, who was Icelandic and lived in Berlin, who scored *The Theory of Everything* (2015) and *Arrival* (2016); and Dario Marinelli, an Italian who lives in London, who scored *Atonement* (2007) and *Darkest Hour* (2017). It is still a challenge, however, to find reliable information about the careers of composers who do not have credentials in Hollywood. Once the spotlight is turned more fully on them, we can hope it will reveal the emergence of women as well as people of color in greater numbers.

Conclusion

Film music had its inception at the beginning of film history, and it continues to be an integral part of film production in the early twenty-first century. Its practice has become virtually indispensable to the marketability of contemporary films throughout the world. Witness the insertion of several songs performed by jazz singer Dianne Reeves into the gritty realism of *Good Night, and Good Luck* (2005), a film that otherwise omits musical accompaniment entirely. Cross-promoted on radio, television, and the Internet and recorded and transmitted in various mediums, soundtracks featuring a film's music now precede a film's release and may produce higher profits than the film itself.

In some ways, film music has come full circle. The advent of the compilation score harkens back to silent film accompaniment with its cue sheets of specific musical references, many of which were to popular song. Musical accompaniment is one of the many ways in which film as an art form is returning to its roots in the late nineteenth and early twentieth centuries when Edison initially envisioned film viewing as an activity taking place in the home, an amalgamation of music and image experienced in the family parlor.

There are new frontiers, too. It is interesting to consider the presence and power of music in television, music videos, video games, and websites. How and why did music become crucial to the ways in which these phenomena operate at least some of the time? Music in film, after all, is functional; it provides very specific qualities to the medium, qualities that film has come to depend on. To what extent do these new media forms depend on music as well? What functions that music provides to film might also prove crucial in these new arenas? At this point, I am not prepared to offer even a "very short" answer. I will leave these and questions like them to others to chart film music's continuing legacy.

References

Chapter 1

Mary Ramos is quoted in David Browne, "Inside Tarantino's *Once Upon a Time in Hollywood* Soundtrack," *Rolling Stone*, July 27, 2019, https://www.rollingstone.com/music/music-features/inside-tarantino-once-upon-a-time-in-hollywood-soundtrack-864276/. Susan Jacobs is quoted in Holly Gordon, "How the Film *Promising Young Woman* Landed Its Pop-Perfect Soundtrack," *CBC.CA* (Radio Canada), January 5, 2021, https://www.cbc.ca/music/how-the-film-promising-young-woman-landed-its-pop-perfect-soundtrack-1.5844149. Guillermo del Toro is quoted in Gina McIntyre, *The Shape of Water: Creating a Fairy Tale for Troubled Times* (San Rafael, CA: Insight Editions, 2017), 141.

Chapter 2

A. R. Rahman is quoted in "10 Questions for A. R. Rahman," *Time*, April 6, 2009, https://content.time.com/time/subscriber/article/0,33009,1887759,00.html.
John Barry is interviewed in the documentary *Dances with Wolves: The Creation of an Epic* (2003). Randy Newman is quoted in Fred Karlin's *Listening to the Movies: The Film Lover's Guide to Film Music* (New York: Schirmer, 1994), 72. Jonny Greenwood is quoted in Alex Ross, "How Jonny Greenwood Wrote the Year's Best Film Score," *The New Yorker*, December 19, 2021, https://www.newyorker.com/culture/the-new-yorker-interview/

how-jonny-greenwood-wrote-the-years-best-film-score. The quote
from Theodor Adorno and Hanns Eisler is from their *Composing
for the Films* (New York: Oxford University Press, 1947; reprint,
London: Athlone Press, 1994), 8.

Claudia Gorbman's quotes come from her *Unheard Melodies:
Narrative Film Music* (Bloomington: Indiana University Press,
1987), 16 and 58. Noël Carroll's quote is from his *Mystifying
Movies: Fads and Fallacies in Contemporary Film Theory* (New
York: Columbia University Pres, 1988), 219. Elmer Bernstein is
quoted in Tony Thomas's *The View from the Podium* (New York:
A. S. Barnes, 1973), 193.

Chapter 3

The quote from Theodor Adorno is from his *Introduction to the
Sociology of Music*, trans. E. B. Ashton (New York: Seabury Press,
1976), 30. The quotes from Theodor Adorno and Hanns Eisler are
from their *Composing for the Films* (New York: Oxford University
Press, 1947; reprint, London: Athlone Press, 1994), 59. The quotes
from Claudia Gorman are from her *Unheard Melodies: Narrative
Film Music* (Bloomington: Indiana University Press, 1987), 58 and
64. The quotes from Caryl Flinn are from her *Strains of Utopia:
Gender, Nostalgia, and Hollywood Film Music* (Princeton, NJ:
Princeton University Press, 1992), 9.

The quote "sonorous envelope of the self" is from Didier Anzieu,
"L'enveloppe sonore du soi," *Nouvelle revue de psychanalyse* 13
(Spring 1976): 161; "sonorous space" is from Gérard Blanchard,
Images de la musique de cinéma (Paris: Edilig, 1984), 95; and
"murmuring house" and "reunited bodies" are from Guy Rosolato,
"La voix: entre corps et langage," *Revue francaise de psychanalyses*
38, no. 1 (January 1974): 81 and 82. All translations from the
French are my own. Daihachi Oguchi is quoted in "Drummer
Promoted Taiko Style," *Los Angeles Times*, July 1, 2008. Ben
Winter's quote is from his "Corporeality, Musical Heartbeats, and
Cinematic Emotion," *Music Sound and the Moving Image* 2, no. 1
(2008): 22.

Chapter 4

Thomas Edison is quoted in Rick Altman, *Silent Film Sound* (New
York: Columbia University Press, 2004), 78. John Bunny is quoted

in Denis Condon, "'Players Must Be of a Good Class': Women and Concert Musicians in Irish Picture Houses, 1910–1920," in *Music and Sound in the Silent Film: From the Nickelodeon to* The Artist, ed. Ruth Barton and Simon Trezise (New York: Routledge, 2019), 86.

Hamid Naficy's quote is from his *A Social History of Iranian Cinema*, vol. 1, *The Artisanal Era: 1897–1941* (Durham, NC: Duke University Press, 2011), 116. Savaş Arslan's quote is from his *Cinema in Turkey: A New Critical History* (New York: Oxford University Press, 2011), 31. "Satirical musical accompaniment" is from Theodore van Houten, *Silent Cinema Music in the Netherlands* (Buren, The Netherlands: Frits Knuf, 1992), 30. "Natural Law" is from *Moving Picture News*, March 19, 1910. The Russian newspaper quotes are from Yuri Tsivian, "The Acoustics of Cinema Performance," in *Early Cinema in Russia and Its Cultural Reception*, ed. Richard Taylor, trans. Alan Bodger (London: Routledge, 1994), 229n44.

Chapter 5

Scott Bradley's quote is from his "Music in Cartoons," in *The Cartoon Music Book*, ed. Daniel Goldmark and Yuval Taylor (Chicago: A Capella, 2002), 118.

Tôru Takemitsu is quoted in Donald Richie's "Notes on the Film Music of Takemitsu Tôru," *Contemporary Music Review* 21, no. 4 (2002): 10. Satyajit Ray's quote is from his *Our Films, Their Films* (New York: Hyperion, 1994), 73.

Chapter 6

Sofia Coppola is quoted in "*Marie Antoinette*: A Coppola Story," *Sartorial Storytelling*, May 1, 2013, https://sartorialstorytelling. wordpress.com/2013/05/01/marie-antoinette-a-coppola-story/. Lynn Fainchtein is quoted in Richard Villegas, "The Music in Alfonso Cuarón's *Roma* Is a Meticulously Accurate Document of 1970s Mexico," Remezcla.com, December 17, 2018, https:// remezcla.com/features/film/music-roma-cuaron/. Hamid Naficy's quote is from his "Islamizing Film Culture in Iran," in *Political Culture in the Islamic Republic*, ed. Samih K. Farsoun and Mehrdad Mashayekhi (London: Routledge, 1992), 182. Tan Dun is quoted in Ian Buruma, "Of Musical Import," *New York Times*,

May 8, 2008. A. R. Rahman is quoted in "10 Questions for A. R. Rahman," *Time*, April 6, 2009, https://content.time.com/time/subscriber/article/0,33009,1887759,00.html.

Chapter 7

Bernard Herrmann's quote is from his "A Lecture on Film Music," in *The Hollywood Film Music Reader*, ed. Mervyn Cooke (New York: Oxford University Press, 2010), 212. Max Steiner's quote comes from his "The Music Director," in *The Real Tinsel*, ed. Bernard Rosenberg and Harry Silverstein (London: Macmillan, 1970), 392. Bernard Herrmann is quoted in George Burt, *The Art of Film Music* (Boston: Northeastern University Press, 1994), 221. Liu Zhuang is quoted in George Semsel, "Liu Zhuang: Composer," in *Chinese Film: The State of the Art in the People's Republic,* ed. George Semsel (New York: Praeger, 1987), 176–77. Philip Glass's quote is from David Morgan, *Knowing the Score: Film Composers Talk About the Art, Craft, Blood, Sweat, and Tears of Writing for Cinema* (New York: HarperCollins, 2000), 238.

John Barry is quoted in Michael Schelle, ed., *The Score: Interviews with Film Composers*, 22. Ennio Morricone's quote is from his "A Composer behind the Film Camera," trans. Elena Boschi, *Music, Sound, and the Moving Image* 1, no. 1 (2007): 98. A. R. Rahman is quoted in S. James Snyder, "A. R. Rahman, *Slumdog Millionaire* Maestro," *Time*, February 5, 2009, https://content.time.com/time/arts/article/0,8599,1876545,00.html. Paul Thomas Anderson is quoted in Madison Brek, "Paul Thomas Anderson, Jonny Greenwood, and the Creative Partnership of the Decade," FSR [Film School Rejects].com, November 29, 2019, https://filmschoolrejects.com/paul-thomas-anderson-jonny-greenwood-decade/. Sergei Eisenstein's quote is from his *Notes of a Film Director*, trans. X. Danko (New York: Dover, 1970), 156. Pablo Larrain is quoted in Ned Beauman, "Mica Levi's Intensely Unconventional Film Scores," *The New Yorker*, February 23, 2017, https://www.newyorker.com/culture/persons-of-interest/mica-levis-anti-musical-soundtracks. Alex North is quoted in David Kraft, "A Conversation with Alex North," *Soundtrack Magazine* 4, no. 13 (1985), 8. Kevin Costner is interviewed in the documentary *Dances with Wolves: The Creation of an Epic* (2003). Ennio Morricone's quote is from his "A Composer behind the Film Camera," trans. Elena Boschi, *Music, Sound, and the Moving*

Image 1, no. 1 (2007): 97. Miklós Rózsa's quotes are from his autobiography, *Double Life* (New York: Hippocrene, 1982), 98 and 126. Bernard Herrmann's quote is from his "A Lecture on Film Music," in *The Hollywood Film Music Reader*, ed. Mervyn Cooke (New York: Oxford University Press, 2010), 212. Alfred Hitchcock is quoted in Jack Sullivan, *Hitchcock's Music* (New Haven, CT: Yale University Press, 2007), 228. Anil Biswas is quoted in Gregory Booth's *Behind the Curtain: Making Music in Mumbai's Film Studios* (New York: Oxford University Press, 2008), 261. Rachel Portman, Georges Delerue, and Jerry Goldsmith are quoted in Fred Karlin's *Listening to Movies: The Film Lover's Guide to Film Music* (New York: Schirmer, 1994), 27 and 28. Philip Glass is quoted in "Variations on the Musical Image: An Interview with Philip Glass," *Documentary Box*, no. 22 (2003), 23. Ramin Djawadi is quoted in "*Game of Thrones* Composer Ramin Djawadi on Melodies That Stick," NPR [National Public Radio], February 14, 2017, https://www.npr.org/2017/02/14/515023088/game-of-thrones-composer-ramin-djawadi-on-melodies-that-stick. Benny Rosario is quoted in Gregory Booth, *Behind the Curtain: Making Music in Mumbai's Film Studios* (New York: Oxford University Press, 2008), 201. Danny Elfman and Steve Bartek are quoted in Janet K. Halfyard's *Danny Elfman's* Batman: *A Film Score Guide* (Lanham, MD: Scarecrow Press, 2004), 12, 15, and 14. James Newton Howard is quoted in Michael Schelle, ed., *The Score: Interviews with Film Composers* (Beverly Hills, CA: Silman–James, 1999), 183.

Valentin Silvestrov is quoted in Anastassia Boutsko, "Ukrainian Composer Valentin Silvestrov: 'What Are You Kremlin Devils Doing?,'" DW [Deutsche Welle].com, March 17, 2022, https://www.dw.com/en/ukrainian-composer-valentin-silvestrov-what-are-you-kremlin-devils-doing/a-61158308. Hans Zimmer is quoted in Felicity Wilcox, ed., *Women's Music for the Screen: Diverse Narratives in Sound* (New York: Routledge, 2022), 133.

Laura Karpman is quoted in Tim Greiving, "Female Composers Are Trying to Break Film's Sound Barrier," *New York Times*, January 10, 2019.

Further reading

Reference guides, handbooks, and online resources

Cooke, Mervyn, and Fiona Ford, eds. *The Cambridge Companion to Film Music*. Cambridge: Cambridge University Press, 2016.

Goldmark, Daniel, ed. *The New Grove Music Guide to American Film Music*. New York: Oxford University Press, 2019.

Kalinak, Kathryn, ed. *Music and Cinema, Global Practices*. Oxford Bibliographies Online, 2017. https://www.oxfordbibliographies.com.

Lee, Jonathan Rhodes, ed. *Music in the Sound Era: A Research and Information Guide*. 2 vols. New York: Routledge, 2020.

Neumeyer, David, ed. *The Oxford Handbook of Film Music Studies*. New York: Oxford University Press, 2014.

Sherk, Warren, ed. *Film and Television Music: A Guide to Books, Articles, and Composer Interviews*. Lanham, MD: Scarecrow Press, 2011.

Film music histories

Cooke, Mervyn. *A History of Film Music*. Cambridge: Cambridge University Press, 2008.

Wierzbicki, James. *Film Music: A History*. New York: Routledge, 2009.

Case studies

Cooper, David. *Bernard Herrmann's* Vertigo: *A Film Score Handbook*. Westport, CT: Greenwood Press, 2001.

Halfyard, Janet K. *Danny Elfman's* Batman: *A Film Score Guide.* Lanham, MD: Scarecrow Press, 2004.

Leinberger, Charles. *Ennio Morricone's* The Good, the Bad, and the Ugly: *A Film Score Guide.* Lanham, MD: Scarecrow Press, 2004.

Wierzbicki, James. *Louis and Bebe Barron's Score for* Forbidden Planet: *A Film Score Guide.* Lanham, MD: Scarecrow Press, 2005.

Winters, Ben. *Erich Wolfgang Korngold's* The Adventures of Robin Hood: *A Film Score Guide.* Lanham, MD: Scarecrow Press, 2007.

Film music theory and analysis

Adorno, Theodor (uncredited in the original English-language edition), and Hanns Eisler. *Composing for the Films.* New York: Oxford University Press, 1947. Reprint, London: Athlone Press, 1994.

Buhler, James. "Ontological, Formal, and Critical Theories of Film Music." In *The Oxford Handbook of Film Music Studies*, edited by David Neumeyer, 188–225. New York: Oxford University Press, 2014.

Buhler, James. "Psychoanalysis, Apparatus Theory, and Subjectivity." In *The Oxford Handbook of Film Music Studies*, edited by David Neumeyer, 383–417. New York: Oxford University Press, 2014.

Carroll, Noël. *Mystifying Movies: Fads and Fallacies in Contemporary Film Theory.* New York: Columbia University Press, 1988.

Chell, Samuel. "Music and Emotion in the Classical Hollywood Film: The Case of *The Best Years of Our Lives.*" *Film Criticism* 8, no. 2 (Winter 1984): 27–38.

Dickinson, Kay. *Off Key: When Film and Music Won't Work Together.* New York: Oxford University Press, 2008.

Eisenstein, Sergei, Vsevolod Pudovkin, and Grigori Alexandrov. "Statement on Sound." In Sergei Eisenstein, *Writings, 1922–1934*, edited by Richard Taylor, 113–14. London: I. B. Taurus, 2010.

Gorbman, Claudia. *Unheard Melodies: Narrative Film Music.* Bloomington: Indiana University Press, 1987.

Heldt, Guido. "Film-Music Theory." In *The Cambridge Companion to Film Music*, edited by Mervyn Cooke and Fiona Ford, 97–113. Cambridge: Cambridge University Press, 2016.

Levinson, Jerrold. "Film Music and Narrative Agency." In *Post-Theory: Reconstructing Film Studies*, edited by David Bordwell and Noël Carroll, 249–82. Madison: University of Wisconsin Press, 1996.

Smith, Jeff. "Unheard Melodies? A Critique of Psychoanalytic Theories of Film Music." In *Post-Theory: Reconstructing Film Studies*, edited by David Bordwell and Noël Carroll, 230–47. Madison: University of Wisconsin Press, 1996.

Winters, Ben. "Corporeality, Musical Heartbeats, and Cinematic Emotion." *Music Sound and the Moving Image* 2, no. 1 (2008): 3–25.

Gender and sexuality in the film score

Buhler, James. "Gender, Sexuality, and the Soundtrack." In *The Oxford Handbook of Film Music Studies*, edited by David Neumeyer, 366–82. New York: Oxford University Press, 2014.

Decker, Todd. "The Musical Mr. Ripley: Closeting a Character in the 1950s and a Film in the 1990s." *Music, Sound, and the Moving Image* 6, no. 2 (2012): 185–208.

Dubowsky, Jack Curtis. *Intersecting Film, Music, and Queerness.* New York: Palgrave Macmillan, 2016.

Flinn, Caryl. *Strains of Utopia: Gender, Nostalgia, and Hollywood Film Music.* Princeton, NJ: Princeton University Press, 1992.

Franklin, Peter. *Seeing through Music: Gender and Modernism in Classic Hollywood Film Scores.* New York: Oxford University Press, 2015.

Haworth, Catherine. "Introduction: Gender, Sexuality, and the Soundtrack." *Music, Sound, and the Moving Image* 6, no. 2 (2012): 113–36.

Haworth, Catherine. "'Something beneath the Flesh': Music, Gender and Medical Discourse in the 1940s Female Gothic Film." *Journal for the Society for American Music* 8, no. 3 (2014): 345.

Haworth, Catherine, ed. "Gender, Sexuality, and the Soundtrack." Special issue, *Music, Sound, and the Moving Image* 6, no. 2 (2012).

Howell, Amanda. *Popular Film Music and Masculinity in Action.* New York: Routledge, 2015.

Laing, Heather. *The Gendered Score: Music in 1940s Melodrama and the Woman's Film.* London: Routledge, 2016.

Lin, Zhichun. "The Heard and Unheard Sounds of Women: A Comparison of Female Silence and Theme Music in Two Versions of *Letter from an Unknown Woman*." *Music and the Moving Image* 5, no. 3 (2012): 11–27.

Mera, Miguel. "Outing the Score: Music, Narrative, and Collaborative Process in *Little Ashes*." *Music, Sound, and the Moving Image* 6, no. 1 (2012): 93–109.

Miranda, Laura. "The Spanish 'Crusader Film': Gender Connotations during the Conflict." *Music, Sound, and the Moving Image* 4, no. 2 (2010): 161–72.

Samer, Roxanne, and William Whittington, eds. *Spectatorship: Shifting Theories of Gender, Sexuality, and the Media*. Austin: University of Texas Press, 2017.

The silent era: 1895–1927

Altman, Rick. *Silent Film Sound*. New York: Columbia University Press, 2004.

Barton, Ruth, and Simon Trezise, eds. *Music and Sound in the Silent Film: From the Nickelodeon to* The Artist. New York: Routledge, 2019.

Carbine, Mary. "'The Finest Outside the Loop': Motion Picture Exhibition in Chicago's Black Metropolis, 1905–1928." In *Silent Film*, edited by Richard Abel, 234–62. New Brunswick, NJ: Rutgers University Press, 1996.

Condon, Denis. "'Players Must Be of a Good Class': Women and Concert Musicians in Irish Picture Houses, 1910–1920." In *Music and Sound in the Silent Film: From the Nickelodeon to* The Artist, edited by Ruth Barton and Simon Trezise, 79–92. New York: Routledge, 2019.

Donnelly, K. J., and Ann-Kristin Wallengren, eds. *Today's Sounds for Yesterday's Films*. New York: Palgrave Macmillan, 2016.

Johnston, Phillip. *Silent Films/Loud Music: New Ways of Listening to and Thinking about Silent Film Music*. New York: Bloomsbury, 2021.

Leonard, Kendra Preston. "Women at the Pedals: Female Cinema Musicians during the Great War." In *Over Here, Over There: Transatlantic Conversations on the Music of World War I*, edited by Williams Brooks, Christina Bashford, and Gayle Magee, 149–73. Urbana: University of Illinois Press, 2019.

Marks, Martin. *Music and the Silent Film: Contexts and Case Studies, 1895–1924*. New York: Oxford University Press, 1997.

Porter, Laraine. "Music, Gender, and the Feminisation of British Silent Cinema, 1909–1929." In *Music and Sound in the Silent Film: From*

the Nickelodeon to The Artist, edited by Ruth Barton and Simon
Trezise, 93–108. New York: Routledge, 2019.

Silent Film Sound & Music Archive: A Digital Repository. https://
www.sfsma.org.

Windisch, Anna K., and Claus Tieber. "'Silent' Films, Singing Voices:
Vocal Accompaniment in Viennese Moving Picture Exhibition,
1913–1923." *Music and the Moving Image* 8, no. 1 (2015): 19–36.

The sound era: 1927–70

Avila, Jacqueline. *Cinesonidos: Film Music and National Identity
during Mexico's Época de oro.* New York: Oxford University
Press, 2019.

Bartig, Kevin. *Composing for the Red Screen: Prokofiev and Soviet
Film.* New York: Oxford University Press, 2014.

Colvin, Michael. *Fado and the Urban Poor in Portuguese Cinema
of the 1930s and 1940s.* Rochester, NY: Tamesis Books, 2016.

Egorova, Tatiana K. *Soviet Film Music: An Historical Survey.*
Translated by Tatiana A. Ganf and Natalia A. Egunova.
Amsterdam: Harwood Academic, 1997.

Flinn, Caryl. *The New German Cinema: Music, History, and the
Matter of Style.* Berkeley: University of California Press, 2004.

Gabbard, Krin. *Jammin' at the Margins: Jazz and the American
Cinema.* Chicago: University of Chicago Press, 1996.

Gil Curiel, Germán. *Film Music in "Minor" National Cinemas.*
New York: Bloomsbury Academic, 2016.

Gil Marino, Cecilia Nuria, and Laura Miranda, eds. *Identity
Mediations in Latin American Cinema and Beyond: Culture,
Music and Transnational Discourses.* Newcastle upon Tyne, UK:
Cambridge Scholars, 2019.

Goldmark, Daniel, and Yuval Taylor, eds. *The Cartoon Music Book.*
Chicago: A Cappella Press, 2002.

Kalinak, Kathryn. *Settling the Score: Music and the Classical
Hollywood Film.* Madison: University of Wisconsin Press, 1992.

Mera, Miguel, and David Burnand, eds. *European Film Music.*
Aldershot, UK: Ashgate, 2006.

Rees, Lucy M. *Mongolian Film Music: Tradition, Revolution, and
Propaganda.* Surrey, UK: Ashgate, 2015.

Shaw, Lisa, and Rob Stone. *Screening Songs in Hispanic and
Lusophone Cinema.* Manchester, UK: Manchester University
Press, 2012.

Stilwell, Robynn J., and Phil Powrie. *Composing for the Screen in Germany and the USSR*. Bloomington: Indiana University Press, 2008.

Titus, Joan. *The Early Film Music of Dimitry Shostakovich*. New York: Oxford University Press, 2016.

Tuohy, Sue. "Metropolitan Sounds: Music in Chinese Films of the 1930s." In *Cinema and Urban Culture in Shanghai, 1922–1943*, edited by Yingjin Zhang, 200–21. Palo Alto, CA: Stanford University Press, 1999.

Yeh, Emilie (Yueh-yu). "Historiography and Sinification: Music in Chinese Cinema of the 1930s." *Cinema Journal* 41, no. 3 (Spring 2002): 78–97.

The sound era: 1970–present

Booth, Gregory. *Behind the Curtain: Making Music in Mumbai's Film Studios*. New York: Oxford University Press, 2008.

Creekmur, Corey K. "Picturizing American Cinema: Hindi Film Songs and the Last Days of Genre." In *Soundtrack Available: Essays on Film and Popular Music*, edited by Pamela Robertson Wojcik and Arthur Knight, 375–406. Durham, NC: Duke University Press, 2001.

Davison, Annette. *Hollywood Theory, Non-Hollywood Practice: Cinema Soundtracks in the 1980s and 1990s*. Aldershot, UK: Ashgate, 2004.

Godsall, Jonathan. *Reeled In: Pre-existing Music in Narrative Film*. London: Routledge, 2019.

Kassabian, Anahid. *Hearing Film: Tracking Identifications in Contemporary Hollywood Film Music*. New York: Routledge, 2001.

Mera, Miguel, and David Burnand, eds. *European Film Music*. Aldershot, UK: Ashgate, 2006.

Romney, Jonathan, and Adrian Wooton, eds. *Celluloid Jukebox: Popular Music and the Movies Since the 50s*. London: British Film Institute, 1995.

Slobin, Mark, ed. *Global Soundtracks: Worlds of Film Music*. Middletown, CT: Wesleyan University Press, 2008.

Smith, Jeff. *The Sounds of Commerce: Marketing Popular Film Music*. New York: Columbia University Press, 1998.

Wojcik, Pamela Robertson, and Arthur Knight, eds. *Soundtrack Available: Essays on Film and Popular Music*. Durham, NC: Duke University Press, 2001.

Composers and score composition

Cooke, Mervyn, ed. *The Hollywood Film Music Reader*. New York: Oxford University Press, 2010.

Gengaro, Christine. *Listening to Stanley Kubrick: The Music in His Films*. Lanham, MD: Rowman & Littlefield, 2014.

Hubai, Gergely. *Torn Music: Rejected Film Scores*. West Hollywood, CA: Silman–James, 2012.

McQuiston, Kate. *We'll Meet Again: Musical Design in the Films of Stanley Kubrick*. New York: Oxford University Press, 2013.

Morgan, David. *Knowing the Score: Film Composers Talk About the Art, Craft, Blood, Sweat, and Tears of Writing for Cinema*. New York: HarperCollins, 2000.

Rawle, Steven, and K. J. Donnelly, eds. *Partners in Suspense: Critical Essays on Bernard Herrmann and Alfred Hitchcock*. Manchester, UK: Manchester University Press, 2017.

Saltzman, Steven A. *The Music of Film: Collaborations and Conversations*. New York: Routledge, 2022.

Schelle, Michael, ed. *The Score: Interviews with Film Composers*. Beverly Hills, CA: Silman–James, 1999.

Schrader, Matt, ed. Score, *A Film Music Documentary: The Interviews*. Los Angeles: Epicleff Media, 2017.

Sullivan, Jack. *Hitchcock's Music*. New Haven, CT: Yale University Press, 2006.

Wilcox, Felicity, ed. *Women's Music for the Screen: Diverse Narratives in Sound*. New York: Routledge, 2022.

Recommended viewing

Chapter 1: What does film music do?

The Shape of Water. 2018. Directed by Guillermo del Toro. Music
supervision by John Houlihan (uncredited).

Chapter 2: How does film music work?

Beauty and the Beast. 1991. Directed by Gary Trousdale and Kirk
Wise. Songs by Howard Ashman and Alan Menken. Score by
Alan Menken.
The Good, the Bad, and the Ugly. 1966. Directed by Sergio Leone.
Score by Ennio Morricone.
Monsoon Wedding. 2001. Directed by Mira Nair. Score by
Mychael Danna.
Psycho. 1960. Directed by Alfred Hitchcock. Score by Bernard
Herrmann.

Chapter 4: A history of film music I: 1895–1927

Silent films exist in a variety of versions with different musical scores
depending on the company issuing the film. The films listed for
this chapter denote the specific score as well as the releasing
company and date of reissue. All were still "in print" as DVDs or
Blu-rays at the time of this edition's publication.
Battleship Potemkin. 1925. Directed by Sergei Eisenstein. Original
score by Edmund Meisel (for the 1926 Berlin premiere). Kino
Lorber, 2010.

Body and Soul. 1925. Directed by Oscar Micheaux. New score by Wycliffe Gordon. Criterion Collection, 2004.

The Cheat. 1915. Directed by Cecil B. DeMille. New score by Robert Israel. With *Carmen.* 1915. Directed by Cecil B. DeMille. Original compilation score (based on Georges Bizet) by Hugo Riesenfeld. Flicker Alley, 2015.

Dickson Experimental Sound Film. 1894/95. Directed by W. K. L. Dickson. https://archive.org/details/dicksonfilmtwo.

Entr-acte. 1924. Directed by Rene Clair. Original score by Erik Satie. Criterion Collection. 2002.

The Man with the Movie Camera. 1929. [*Dziga Vertov: The Man with the Movie Camera and Other Newly-Restored Works.*] New score by Alloy Orchestra. With *Kino-Eye.* 1924. Directed by Dziga Vertov. New score by Robert Israel. Flicker Alley, 2015.

Metropolis. 1927. Directed by Fritz Lang. Original score by Gottfried Huppertz. Kino Lorber, 2010.

Metropolis. [*Giorgio Moroder Presents Metropolis.*] New score by Giorgio Moroder. Kino Lorber, 2011.

The New Babylon. 1929. Directed by Grigori Kozintsev and Leonid Trauberg. Original score by Dmitri Shostakovich. Eccentric Press, 2005.

Nosferatu. 1922. Directed by F. W. Murnau. Original score by Hans Erdmann. Kino Lorber, 2013.

La Roue. 1923. Directed by Abel Gance. New score by Robert Israel. Flicker Alley, 2008.

Sherlock Jr. 1924. Directed by Buster Keaton. With *Three Ages.* New orchestral scores by Mont Alto Motion Picture Orchestra and Clubfoot Orchestra and a compilation score by Jay Ward. Kino Lorber, 2010.

Chapter 5: A history of film music II: 1927–1970

The Adventures of Robin Hood. 1938. Directed by Michael Curtiz and William Keighley. Score by Erich Wolfgang Korngold.

Aguirre: Wrath of God. 1972. Directed by Werner Herzog. Score by Popol Vuh.

Apu Trilogy: *Pather Panchali,* 1955; *Aparajito,* 1956; *The World of Apu,* 1960. Directed by Satyajit Ray. Scores by Ravi Shankar.

Awara. 1951. Directed by Raj Kapoor. Score by Shankar–Jaikishan (Shankar Raghuwanshi and Jaikishan Pankal).

Deserter. 1934. Directed by Vsevolod Pudovkin. Score by Yuri Shaporin.

Elevator to the Gallows. 1958. Directed by Louis Malle. Score by Miles Davis.

The Good, the Bad, and the Ugly. 1966. Directed by Sergio Leone. Score by Ennio Morricone.

King Kong. 1933. Directed by Merian C. Cooper and Ernst Schoedsack. Score by Max Steiner.

Kwaidan. 1965. Directed by Masaki Kobayashi. Score by Tŏru Takemitsu.

Let's Go with Pancho Villa! 1936. Directed by Fernando de Fuentes. Score by Silvestre Revueltas.

Rashomon. 1950. Directed by Akira Kurosawa. Score by Fumio Hayasaka.

Rebel without a Cause. 1955. Directed by Nicolas Ray. Score by Leonard Rosenman.

Steamboat Willie. 1928. Produced by Walt Disney. Score uncredited.

Street Angel. 1937. Directed by Muzhi Yuan. Score by Luting He.

Ugetsu. 1953. Directed by Kenji Mizoguchi. Score by Fumio Hayasaka.

Vivre sa vie. 1962. Directed by Jean-Luc Godard. Score by Michel Legrand.

Wuthering Heights. 1939. Directed by William Wyler. Score by Alfred Newman.

Zéro de conduit. 1933. Directed by Jean Vigo. Score by Maurice Jaubert.

Chapter 6: A history of film music III: 1970–2022

Baby Driver. 2017. Directed by Edgar Wright. Score by Steven Price. Music supervision by Kirsten Lane.

Bladerunner. 1982. Directed by Ridley Scott. Score by Vangelis.

Chungking Express. 1994. Directed by Wong Kar-wai. Original music by Fan-kei Chan, Michael Galasso, and Roel A. Garcia.

Crouching Tiger, Hidden Dragon. 2000. Directed by Ang Lee. Score by Tan Dun.

Dune. 2021. Directed by Denis Villeneuve. Score by Hans Zimmer.

Forbidden Planet. 1956. Directed by Fred M. Wilcox. Electronic tonalities by Bebe Barron and Louis Barron.

Half Moon. 2006. Directed by Bahman Ghobadi. Score by Hossein Alizadeh.

Her. Directed by Spike Jonze. 2013. Score by Arcade Fire.

The Kite Runner. 2007. Directed by Marc Forster. Score by Alberto Iglesias.

Lagaan: Once upon a Time in India. 2001. Score by A. R. Rahman.

Ran. 1985. Directed by Akira Kurosawa. Score by Tōru Takemitsu.

Roma. 2018. Directed by Alfonso Cuarón. Music supervision by Lynn Fainchtein.

Slumdog Millionaire. 2008. Directed by Danny Boyle. Score by A. R. Rahman.

Star Wars trilogy. *Star Wars* [aka *The New Hope*]. 1977. Directed by George Lucas. *The Empire Strikes Back.* 1980. Directed by Irvin Kershner. *Return of the Jedi.* 1983. Directed by Richard Marquand. Scores by John Williams.

Thelma and Louise. 1991. Directed by Ridley Scott. Score by Hans Zimmer. Music supervision by Kathy Nelson.

The Thin Blue Line. 1988. Directed by Errol Morris. Score by Philip Glass.

Chapter 7: Composers and their craft

Alexander Nevsky. 1938. Directed by Sergei Eisenstein. Score by Sergei Prokofiev.

Batman. 1989. Directed by Tim Burton. Score by Danny Elfman.

Dances with Wolves. 1990. Directed by Kevin Costner. Score by John Barry.

Dances with Wolves: The Creation of an Epic. 2003. Directed by J. M. Kenney. With John Barry.

Encanto. 2021. Directed by Jared Bush and Byron Howard. Score by Germaine Franco.

Gladiator. 2000. Directed by Ridley Scott. Score by Hans Zimmer and Lisa Gerrard.

Joker. 2019. Directed by Todd Phillips. Score by Hildur Guðnadóttir.

One Night in Miami. 2020. Directed by Regina King. Score by Terence Blanchard.

A Quiet Place. 2018. Directed by John Krasinski. Score by Marco Beltrami.

Soul. 2020. Directed by Pete Docter and Kemp Powers. Score by Trent Reznor, Atticus Ross, and Jon Batiste.

Spellbound. 1945. Directed by Alfred Hitchcock. Score by Miklós Rózsa.

There Will Be Blood. 2007. Directed by Paul Thomas Anderson. Score by Jonny Greenwood.

2001: A Space Odyssey. 1968. Directed by Stanley Kubrick. Score uncredited.

Under the Skin. 2013. Directed by Jonathan Glazer. Score by Mica Levi.

Vertigo. 1958. Directed by Alfred Hitchcock. Score by Bernard Herrmann.

Index

Figures and boxes are indicated by an italic *f* and *b* following the paragraph number.

Index

Film Music

FILM
A Very Short Introduction
Michael Wood

Film is considered by some to be the most dominant art form of the twentieth century. It is many things, but it has become above all a means of telling stories through images and sounds. The stories are often offered to us as quite false, frankly and beautifully fantastic, and they are sometimes insistently said to be true. But they are stories in both cases, and there are very few films, even in avant-garde art, that don't imply or quietly slip into narrative. This story element is important, and is closely connected with the simplest fact about moving pictures: they do move. In this *Very Short Introduction* Michael Wood provides a brief history and examination of the nature of the medium of film, considering its role and impact on society as well as its future in the digital age.

EARLY MUSIC
A Very Short Introduction
Thomas Forrest Kelly

The music of the medieval, Renaissance, and baroque periods
have been repeatedly discarded and rediscovered ever since
they were new. In recent years interest in music of the past
has taken on particular meaning, representing two specific
trends: first, a rediscovery of little-known underappreciated
repertories, and second, an effort to recover lost performing
styles. In this VSI, Thomas Forrest Kelly frames chapters on
the forms, techniques, and repertories of the medieval,
Renaissance, and baroque periods with discussion of why old
music has been and should be revived, along with a short
history of early music revivals.

www.oup.com/vsi